Clematis

Clematis

by

Christopher Lloyd

LONDON

Country Life Limited

First published in 1965
by Country Life Limited
Tower House, Southampton St. W.C.2
Printed in Great Britain by
Billing & Sons Limited
Guildford and London

© *Christopher Lloyd 1965*

Second impression 1966

Contents

5

Acknowledgments

Acknowledgments are due to the following for permission to use photographs in this book: Colour plates 1, 3, 4, 5, 6, 7, *Country Life*; colour plate 2, A. J. Huxley; plates 1, 2, 27, 33, *Country Life*; 3, 4, 6, 7, 8, 9, 10, 11, 12, 13, 14, 15, 16, 17, 18, 19, 20, 22, 23, 24, 29, 31, 32, 34, 36, 37, *Amateur Gardening*; 5, 28, 30, Donald F. Merrett; 21, 25, 35, Christopher Lloyd; 26, H. Smith.

Illustrations

DIAGRAMS

Preface

Writing a book on clematis has been a labour of love. The group has fascinated me ever since I was a small boy and I started collecting them at the age of twelve. I have been lucky enough to be able to continue gardening in the same place, at Great Dixter, ever since, and I believe that some of my clematis plants include a few of those originals. Certainly a number of them are now rising thirty years old, and still going strong.

Ten years ago, my friend John Treasure and I decided to collect all the hardy clematis in cultivation. He, gardening in south Shropshire, and I in East Sussex have worked hand in glove at this, freely exchanging material all along the line. We have still a long way to go, but we are not doing too badly, and we have had enormous fun in trying clematis in every sort of situation that a garden offers. It was his idea, for instance, to use them as a net-work among low, ground-covering heathers.

To him and also to his adjutant, young Raymond Evison, who will one day, I guess, know more about clematis than anyone in the world, I owe a very great debt of gratitude. Whenever I lacked material for describing the varieties, I turned to them and they either sent it me or supplied me with data. They could not have been more co-operative. So has everyone else been, of whom I have sought help. I would also like to thank Captain Lucas of Broomhall, near Horsham, Sussex, for allowing the photographs of Lady Northcliffe, Jackmanii alba, Countess of Lovelace and Barbara Jackman to be taken; Sir George and Lady Jessel for the picture of *C. chrysocoma* on Ladham House, Goudhurst, Kent; and Sir John and Lady Mann for that of Mme Baron-Veillard flowering, in September, on a north wall at Thelveton Hall, Norfolk.

C.L.

9

Part 1

1

Why We Grow Clematis

If we ask ourselves why a plant is popular, we are liable to find that it is for reasons of which we cannot wholly approve. Why, for instance, is *Forsythia intermedia spectabilis* ubiquitous? Obviously, because it carries more bright yellow per cubic inch (and not a leaf to dilute the effect) than any other shrub then flowering. A few weeks later, the double pink cherry, Kanzan, will perform the same kind office, while in July there will be thousands of porches up and down the country loaded with lumps of solid purple, which is *Clematis* Jackmanii. The fastidious gardener shudders in the face of such repetitious vulgarity.

But he would be an anaemic kind of prig if his squeamishness led him to veto the entire race of large-flowered clematis hybrids on the same grounds. Colour in quantity is only objectionable if slapped on with an undiscriminating disregard for texture and form. The fundamental beauty of the finest clematis rests on the exquisite structure of their blooms. No matter how often they are repeated, their individuality will be retained.

Taking the variety Lasurstern as an example: each bloom, at the plant's first flowering in May and June, has a 6- to 7-in. span. And there are seven or eight sepals, which broadly overlap towards the centre of the flower, thus giving it a firm, strong axis. Gradually these radiating sepals taper to very fine points while their margins gently undulate in seductive ripples. The colour is dissatisfying only when we try to describe it, for neither 'blue' nor 'mauve' will do: it is somewhere in between, intense and deep at the flower's first opening, gradually fading to a typical campanula shade. A cushion of prominent stamens in creamy-white form a distinctive

11

focal 'eye'. On a healthy, well-trained plant, more than 200 of these blooms will be repeated over an area 15 ft. wide by 8 ft. high. Combine this fabulous backcloth with a foreground planting of something like *Hemerocallis flava*, with heads of clear yellow trumpets, and the impact is triumphant.

Many varieties are just as well constructed as Lasurstern. But it would be a mistake to assume that those with small flowers are any less enchanting, in their way. The tiny white cruciform blossoms of *C. flammula* are assembled in a seething foam from which flecks spray off at the margins as though the whole mass were really in turbulent motion. Whereas the gay yellow lanterns of *C. orientalis* will shine like a galaxy from the gloom of a sullen north aspect.

Accepted that their outline is always more or less regular, we find an endlessly fascinating diversity of form in different clematis, always satisfying in the species; not always, but often so in the hybrids. And the range of colour which they embrace is no less extensive. Pure blue is never achieved, but we have every gradation of lavender, lilac, indigo, purple and violet. The lilacs lead us towards pink, although this is seldom sufficiently clear (exceptionally, in Duchess of Albany) for the word 'mauve' not to hover in one's thoughts. Neither is pure red available, with the possible exception of some strains of *C. texensis*. We speak and write freely of red clematis, but there is always a little blue in them so that they are more properly crimson or magenta. Then there are chrome-yellow clematis, but only, so far, as small-flowered species. In the palest shades we find cream, grey, skimmed-milk blue-grey and, last but not least, those magnificent albinos which can win converts even among that strange clique of gardeners which dislikes white flowers.

'When shall we come to see your clematis at their best?' is a frequent question which always leaves me vainly fumbling for an easy answer. Because, even while ignoring the one or two odd winter-flowering species, their season is seven months long, and some clematis will be at their peak at one time, some at another.

The varieties of *C. macropetala* and *C. alpina* set the ball rolling in April, together with two evergreen species: *C. indivisa* and *C. armandii*. These overlap into May and are quickly joined by *C. montana* and *C. chrysocoma*. Half-way through the month there starts the season of the largest of the large-flowered hybrids: those which bloom on short laterals off the previous year's shoots. Their first flush lasts till the latter days of June, and included among them we find many with double, rosette-shaped flowers, each packed with scores of sepals. Others, again, are only semi-double. These early-summer-flowering hybrids often bear a second, sometimes even a third, crop at the tips of their young shoots in later summer. The double types, at their reappearance, have mysteriously become single and look altogether different though no less pleasing.

From mid-June onwards the Jackmanii-type clematis and many of the more typical hybrids of *C. viticella* start their season. They have only one flush of bloom but it is very prolonged, as first the terminal buds open and then the laterals. Mme Baron-Veillard is later than most, blooming from August, while Lady Betty Balfour is the latest of all the large-flowered cultivars, with a September season. Meanwhile the yellow *C. orientalis* and *C. tangutica* have opened their season in early July and will continue till the frosts of autumn. *C. flammula* and *C. rehderiana* are August-September-flowering while *C. paniculata*, so popular in America, tends to miss the boat in our cool climate and to be spoilt before it has fairly got going, in October.

This résumé gives a general picture of what the different types of clematis will do for us over a protracted flowering season. The many ways in which they can, thanks to their widely varying habits of growth, be used in different parts of the garden shall be dealt with in detail later.

There remains the question of hardiness, for a plant which is less than fully hardy loses nine-tenths of its attraction for the amateur gardener. Well, nearly all the clematis in cultivation are hardy in Britain; they need no sort of protection, even when quite young, from frost or from wind. They will thrive to the very edge of the sea coast, where salt-laden gales are continually striking them. The time when they really will suffer from high winds is when they are in full bloom: their flowers can then get sadly battered. So can young shoots in spring, if they happen to catch brutal winds just then. The evergreen species are less hardy, but very few of these are worth having.

There seem to me to be many excellent arguments for growing more clematis in all our gardens. But it is, I think, only sensible to ponder once in a while on what may be said against such a plan:

the next chapter is devoted to this rather sombre theme. In the meantime let us remember that, whatever may be argued against them, there are already a great many clematis doing extremely well in a great many gardens. Furthermore they are, more often than not, stunningly beautiful, in their season. The clematis is more popular today than ever before, and it has won this high regard by its own solid merits. Its future is assured because it is a plant for the intelligent gardener and, despite the gradual disappearance of the professional, gardeners are becoming more intelligent. Clematis respond supremely to the magic touch of 'green fingers'. And there is nothing more magical about green fingers than a realisation on their owner's part that a plant is a living thing and will respond to a sympathetic appreciation of its needs.

2

The Other Side of the Picture

'What a hideous sight clematis are at this time of the year!' I remarked to my friend, pointing to a Jackmanii in its full December rig of twisted stems and blackened foliage. 'If you ask me, they're hideous for most of the year', he replied acidly. This pulled me up sharpish, but it is certainly true that clematis plants have no shape of their own. Like many climbers they live as opportunists, grasping at whatever support is handy and rising to the surface and the light where they can reach it. There they flower, seed, and then slump into repose, attired in disreputable scarecrow garb. Well, there it is, and we can anyway mend matters by a little discreet pruning at the earliest opportunity. And let us not forget that roses, whether bush or climbing, look every bit as villainous in their off-season. If gardeners can be blind to this fault in their No. 1 favourite, they can be blind to it in clematis, and so, indeed, most of them are.

Another handicap under which many clematis cultivars labour, and often quite unnecessarily, can be their names. An attractive name is a tremendous asset. How much better Gipsy Queen or Guiding Star than Hagley Hybrid, Mrs P. B. Truax or Mrs N. Thompson; yet the latter sort of name is given to a disproportionately high number of clematis. Obviously it is flattering to have a plant called after one, but this hardly compensates for the fact that a person's name is likely to mean nothing to ninety-nine per cent of the gardeners who might be interested in the plant. There are exceptions, of course. A foreign-sounding name, especially when French (e.g., Mme Edouard André), has its cachet for a certain style of customer, while a British title such as Lady Betty Balfour or Duchess of Sutherland can be even more appealing.

But the main brake on the increased popularity of clematis is crystallised in the three-worded rumour that they are 'difficult to

grow'. And there are germs of truth in this stigma. On light soils
which dry out quickly, they need more than average understanding
and attention. Then, again, quite a lot of nursery stock is put on
the market while still much too small and weak. The late Tom Hay,
one-time superintendent of London's Central Royal Parks and one
of the finest plantsmen of his day, used to declare that he would
never buy a clematis until its stem was the thickness of a pencil.
This would suppose a three-year-old plant at the least. Nowadays
we could never acquire such a veteran—it would either have been
sold long since or have become so hopelessly pot-bound that its
growth was merely marking time. But this is not to say that we
should be content with the miserable wisps that are sometimes
offered. Much the best scheme, whenever possible, is to visit a
specialist clematis nursery in person and choose one's own plants.
Those which are tallest are not necessarily the best. Young
clematis often have a way of outgrowing their strength (whatever
this may mean). A sturdy plant with perhaps only two or three
pairs of leaves, but with a nice tough stem, is much to be pre-
ferred. Nothing is so off-putting as to feel that one is battling with
a hospital case from the outset.

The mysterious fungus disease called 'wilt', which is most liable
to attack young plants, is a further reason for the large-flowered
hybrid clematis being sometimes considered difficult. This is
discussed more fully in the chapter on clematis troubles, but it may
be said straightaway that as so little work has been done on the
disease, practically nothing is known about it, and therefore professional and amateur growers suffer with equal helplessness from
its capricious sallies on their plants.

One last irritation must be vented here. A monstrously high
proportion of clematis are sold wrongly named. If we are sold a
red cultivar when we had ordered a white, the mistake is obvious
enough. But if for one variety ordered we are sent another of the
same colour without being informed of the substitution, we can
easily remain deceived on this question of identity for years; and
this, for anyone taking an intelligent interest in the genus, is a
serious matter.

Much nursery stock is hopelessly muddled. Every nurseryman
must start out by buying in his varieties and they do not come to
him with a badge of authenticity. Many thousands of plants are
imported wholesale from Holland each year, but these are quite

1. *C. patens* (from
Spingarn's Check List).
Mauve-lilac.

2. *C. lanuginosa* (from
Spingarn's Check List).
Pale lavender.

3. Lasurstern. Rich, deep blue fading to campanula blue.

as confused as our own stocks. The British nurseryman is likely to resell before he has had a chance of verifying the plant's identity. It is, moreover, terribly easy (I write from experience) to get stock mixed up in one's own nursery, and if this happens to plants being used for propagation, the error is rapidly multiplied. A nurseryman with a 'botanical eye' can often recognise his varieties by their foliage, without seeing their flowers, so that he will spot a rogue plant mixed in where it should not be. But he cannot be sure of correcting all such errors; and anyhow, most propagators will rely on their labels unquestioningly. A further difficulty arises from the fact that a high proportion of nursery stock never flowers. Those plants required for propagation are discouraged from making flowering wood, as it is no use for the job in hand. And young plants will generally be sold before they have had a chance to prove their identity by blooming. So there is, again, no check.

Anyway, how is one to prove the identity of a clematis which is known or suspected to be wrongly labelled? I do not know all the varieties by sight. I know all those I grow in my garden and a number more besides, but not all the varieties in cultivation, and there is not an expert in the country who is in this desirable position. All one can do is to collect, sift and weigh the evidence from every possible quarter. Descriptions in books might be thought to offer useful evidence, but here again one must be extremely wary. In most cases they are simply copied one from another, not from the plant itself, and the original description must often have been based on recollection, while the author sat writing (as I am) by his winter's fireside. Recollection, even in tranquillity, of a flower's appearance is apt to be alarmingly innaccurate, Even Spingarn, the great American authority on clematis between the wars, amazes by describing Lucie Lemoine as double purple, although it is universally known to be a double white variety.

Quite apart from all such misrepresentation, which is after all purely accidental, many sales of clematis under the wrong title (as of other plants also, of course, particularly roses) would seem to be connived at by the nurseryman for his own convenience. When I ordered Lady Caroline Nevill from a specialist firm, I was served under this title with what turned out to be Lord Nevill, and for Fairy Queen I received Gipsy Queen. It was an artistic touch, I thought, to get the name half right even though the clematis was utterly different!

B

3

Botanical-Historical

Anyone can turn up the technical definition of *Clematis* in a
British Flora or in a dictionary of gardening. Here I should
like to draw attention, in more or less untechnical language, to
some of the points about the genus which seem to me of interest.

It belongs to the family *Ranunculaceae*, which includes many
good garden plants, some of which cannot help but remind us, in
their flowers, of clematis. A panicle of *Thalictrum dipterocarpum*
in full bloom, for instance, could almost be a small-flowered
clematis; while single anemones are strongly reminiscent of the
larger flowered types. A further similarity between this and other
members of the family such as *Caltha* (king-cup), *Thalictrum* and
Anemone is that the perianth is undifferentiated into petals and
sepals but is all of one piece much as are lilies, narcissi and alliums.
In the case of *Clematis* we are fortunately not expected to talk
about its perianth segments every time we refer to the showy,
coloured portion of the flower. It is generally assumed that the
petals are missing and that the sepals (pronounced with a short ĕ,
like pĕt′als) are what remain.

The fruits of a clematis are worthy of note since the styles which
surmount them have continued to grow after the flower's fading
and often contribute a pleasing effect as the seeds ripen. In our
native *C. vitalba*, the styles become feathery and pale grey, and
are aptly known as Old Man's Beard. This featheriness materially
helps in the seeds' distribution when they are eventually blown
from their anchorage. In *C. tangutica*, a succession of blooms is
produced over such a long period that we get a telling conjunction
of flowers and fluffy seed heads intermingled. In *C. viorna*, no
fluffiness is apparent, but the green styles become so prominent
that one might be looking at a colony of exotic spiders, each with
rather more than its fair quota of legs.

18

Clematis are exceptional, in this family, for being mainly (though not always) woody, where the other members of the *Ranunculaceae* are herbaceous. Most clematis (though, again, not all) are climbers, and their leaf stalks (petioles) are adapted, for this purpose, to twist round any suitable aids for support with which they come into contact.

There are said to be some 230 species of clematis, of cosmopolitan distribution but concentrated for the most part in the cool, temperate, northern hemisphere. The majority are deciduous, but some of the less hardy species from warmer climates are evergreen. Nine of these hail from New Zealand and an interesting point relative to this little nucleus is that they are all dioecious (male and female flowers on separate plants) whereas most clematis are hermaphrodite.

We have two New Zealand species in circulation here—*C. indivisa* and *C. afoliata*—which shall be described in their place. They are male forms. The latter is evergreen in a rather special sense for, as its name implies, its foliage is reduced to nothing but a tendril and all its photosynthesis is accomplished by evergreen stems.

There has at times been a move among certain systematic botanists to split two sections of the genus *Clematis* off into separate genera: *Atragene* and *Viorna*. The former includes *C. alpina* and its Chinese equivalent, *C. macropetala*. It differs from other clematis in the petal-like processes (petaloid staminodes) located between the flower's real stamens and its sepals, and which give a characteristic and charming double effect. *C. viorna* is characterised by an urn-shaped flower in which the four sepals are separate at the base but are joined at the urn's waist, near its mouth. The near-scarlet *C. texensis* is typical, and through being crossed with Jackmanii-type hybrids gave rise to a race of unusual looking but delightful cultivars, having blooms shaped like lily-flowered tulips in glowing shades of pink and red.

However, *Atragene* and *Viorna* are still included with *Clematis* in most works of reference, and are so here.

Although grown in English gardens from the end of the sixteenth century, little interest was taken in clematis until they began to be crossed and 'improved' in the 1850s. Thereafter, for the next twenty years, an extraordinary spate of hybridising activity was let loose throughout Western Europe, and a large proportion of the clematis we know today were created in those years. They derived from three Far Eastern and one (or two) European species. The three Orientals (none of which, alas, is available now) are *C. florida*, *C. patens* and *C. lanuginosa*. They all stem from China, but the first two had long been known in Japanese gardens and had already been considerably hybridised before their introduction into Europe. Thunberg brought *C. florida* in 1776, but this was most probably the double form, *plena*, with greenish-white petaloid stamens. Volume 22 of *Curtis's Botanical Magazine*, published in 1805, is of this opinion. 'We have never seen it with single flowers till very lately', it declares.[1]

The flowers of *C. florida* measured up to $3\frac{1}{2}$ in. across, with four to six sepals; those of *C. patens* (syn. *C. coerulea*), 4 to 6 in. across, with six to eight sepals. The latter was found by Siebold in a Japanese garden and introduced in 1836. Its colour is said to have ranged between white and violet-blue. Whether the true species has ever been seen by European eyes seems doubtful. A number of hybrids between *C. florida* and *C. patens* were brought into Europe from Japan at the time that the first European crosses were being made.

What really set this ball rolling was the introduction in 1850 of *C. lanuginosa* by Robert Fortune, who was collecting for the Royal Horticultural Society in the province of Chekiang, at the most eastern tip of China. His memorandum on the subject is worth quoting: 'This pretty species was discovered at a place called Tein-tung, near the city of Ningpo. It is there wild on the hill-sides, and generally plants itself in light stony soil near the roots of dwarf shrubs, whose stems furnish it with support as it grows. Before the flowering season arrives it has reached the top of the brushwood, and its fine star-shaped, azure blossoms are then seen from a considerable distance rearing themselves proudly above the shrubs to which it had clung for support during its growth. In this state it is most attractive, and well repays any one who is bold enough to scramble through the brushwood to get a nearer view.' The flowers of *C. lanuginosa* are the largest of any species, up to 8 in. across, composed of six to eight sepals.

Turning now to the European scene, the species of prime importance for breeding work was *C. viticella*, from Southern Europe, with purple flowers, only 1 to 2 in. across, composed of four

---

[1] The well-known *C. florida bicolor* (syn. *C. sieboldii*) of our gardens, with *purple* staminodes, was introduced by Siebold in 1837.

4. *C. macropetala* (lavender with blue margins) in a large Ali-Baba jar.

5. *C. macropetala* (close-up).

6. Lady Northcliffe. Deep, slightly richer blue than Lasurstern.

7. Barbara Jackman. Bluish-purple with vivid magenta bar.

obovate (broadest nearer the tip than the base) sepals, hanging lantern-like and never opening flat. It was introduced in the late sixteenth century. The first recorded clematis cross was made between this and, supposedly, *C. integrifolia*, a herbaceous European species. This occurred in Mr Henderson's nursery at St John's Wood in 1835. Actually, *C. integrifolia* was never proved to be the other parent, but judging by results it seems highly probable. *C. integrifolia*, as its name implies, has perfectly simple ovate leaves; it possesses no climbing adaptations whatever and its offspring resembles it in both these respects. It is probably correct to call this cross *C.* × *eriostemon*, but it has also been known variously as *C. hendersonii*, *C. bergeronii*, *C. chandleri* and *C.* × *intermedia*. Twenty-seven years later it was to achieve (relative) immortality by becoming a parent of *C.* Jackmanii, but *C.* × *eriostemon* is still well worth growing for itself; some of the more perverse of us may even prefer it.

Isaac Anderson-Henry of Edinburgh made the first cross using large-flowered, Far Eastern parent blood, namely *C. lanuginosa* and *C. patens*, in 1855. In the following years he brought out many of the largest of the large-flowered hybrids. Lawsoniana, for instance (still listed, but nearly always incorrectly), carries blooms up to 9 in. across. All these were in pale colours. Jackman's of Woking, using *C. viticella* and *C.* × *eriostemon* as well as the Far Eastern clematis achieved cultivars of deeper, more intense colouring, but at the expense of size, and this was Anderson-Henry's experience too, when he attempted to bring depth of colour into his pale-faced whoppers. Even today we can, I think, note the same tendency for size to be correlated with pale shading.

From a cross made between *C.* × *eriostemon* and *C. lanuginosa* in 1858, *C.* Jackmanii was first exhibited in 1863 and caused a sensation.[1] Everyone wanted to grow it, just as everyone wanted to grow *Lilium auratum* on its first appearance from Japan at just this time. From now on, nurserymen throughout Western Europe busied themselves in turning out new varieties. Mr A. G. Jackman

[1] There is, I think, no need to treat seriously Lavallée's claim, made in his monograph *Les Clématites à Grandes Fleurs*, 1884, that Jackmanii was in fact a species, *C. hakonensis*, received by him from Japan. For one thing Jackmanii is patently close to *C. viticella*, and there are no clematis species resembling this in the Far East. For another, Lavallée writes of his *C. hakonensis* as always bearing numerous seeds, which hardly tallies with the habitual sterility of Jackmanii.

criticised some of the Continental hybrids for having long, narrow sepals, but when we consider this character in the twisted segments of a variety such as Mme Jules Corrévon, we may decide that there is a place for clematis of this sort as well as for those with broad, overlapping sepals.

Two names which recur again and again in accounts during this hybridisers' heyday are *C*. Standishii and *C*. Fortunei. They were not species, however, and authorities disagree on the identity of their parents. Often they are given as varieties of *C. patens*. By some, Standishii is considered to be a cross between *C. patens* and *C. florida*. Fortunei, which is of altogether greater interest, almost certainly owes its characters mainly to *C. florida*. For wherever we find doubling of the flowers, we can be confident (where the large-flowered types are in question) that *C. florida* was responsible. Fortunei had very numerous, rather narrow sepals, creamy-white ageing to pale pink. It was, moreover, scented—an attribute to which no attention was paid by the breeders, but which was, nevertheless, passed on to certain offspring, notably The Queen and Fair Rosamond, both of which are with us to this day. Moore and Jackman described this fragrance aptly, I think, as 'intermediate between that of violets and primroses' and exhaled when in a warm, sunny atmosphere.

Certain distinguishing features in the parent species which show up again in the hybrids will be of interest to clematis maniacs. It has already been said that double flowers are derived from *C. florida*. Another character possessed by this species alone is the two leaf-like bracts located half way along the flower stalks (pedicels). The leaves in *C. lanuginosa* are sometimes simple, sometimes ternate (in three leaflets). It is the first condition which is noteworthy, for in *C. patens*, *C. florida* and *C. viticella* the leaves are always compound, with three or more leaflets.

Clematis florida and *C. patens* flower on short laterals from the previous season's wood, in early summer. *C. lanuginosa*, *C. viticella* and *C. integrifolia* all flower on the new season's shoots from midsummer till autumn. The flowers of *C. viticella* and *C. integrifolia* do not open out flat; the sepals are held obliquely. But in all three of the Far Eastern species they open wide. Finally, a distinguishing feature between the flowers of *C. lanuginosa* and those of *C. patens* (see Plates 1 and 2) is that in the former the sepals overlap widely whereas in the latter there are gaps between them.

As may well be imagined, these characters are thoroughly mixed up in the hybrids. From the gardener's point of view, there are only two things which he wants to learn from all this: when any given clematis will flower and (arising from this) how it should be pruned. The nurserymen and other specialists have hence evolved a most complicated, contradictory and confusing system of classification wherewith to help the amateur. They refer each clematis to a group, viz. Lanuginosa, Patens, Florida, Jackmanii, Viticella 1 (large flowered) and Viticella 2 (small flowered)—and then give a pruning system for the group. There is, however, no sense in dragging in an arbitrary pseudo-botanical classification of this kind. It helps nobody and has no validity. Many clematis simply will not conform to it. 'Ville de Lyon' will flower first on its old wood and then on its young, but is dubbed Viticella 1. Marie Boisselot does the same, but is called Lanuginosa, while Proteus starts with enormously double flowers on its old wood but later carries single flowers on the young shoots. This we sometimes find classified as Florida, sometimes Lanuginosa. However, I am glad to be able to say that this crazy system is gradually being discarded.

By 1880, the initial enthusiasm for producing new clematis hybrids had largely spent itself. The baneful effects of 'wilt' disease, then known as 'dying off', were partly responsible; partly it was because every conceivable permutation had been tried in the crossing of the material available, and any startling new developments seemed to be ruled out. True, in the last few years of the century, Jackman's introduced the blood of *C. texensis* (syn. *C. coccinea*), with urn-shaped flowers, by crossing it with Jackmanii, Star of India and others. The result was a race of almost wholly herbaceous climbers, making 12 ft. of growth annually and with masses of smallish bell-shaped blossoms in late summer and autumn. Unfortunately they never really caught on and several have dropped out of the lists. In part this was, I feel, because they do not generally lend themselves well to exhibition, so that they could not become widely known. Also they can get mildew rather badly, though they are little troubled by 'wilt'.

A trickle of new large-flowered varieties continued until the present day. Lasurstern appeared in 1906, Lady Betty Balfour in 1913. Very little went on between the wars, Ernest Markham being alone of note. Lately there has been a moderate renewal of interest in new hybrids, but it is a pity that they should nearly all be early summer flowering. One can, of course, understand that this fits in well with the Chelsea Flower Show's use as a shop window. Furthermore, the early-flowering clematis ripen their seed more readily before winter sets in than do the later types, and this again must influence the breeder's choice of parent material.

Barbara Dibley is exceptional for the intensity of its petunia-red colouring in a huge flower of Nelly Moser type. Vyvyan Pennell has a really good constitution and a great lavender *cum* lilac, double flower of excellent shape. Others of these early-flowering newcomers have regrettably weak constitutions: e.g., Bees' Jubilee, Lincoln Star and Percy Picton. But the outstanding post-war clematis is unquestionably Hagley Hybrid—of exquisite shape and dusky pink colouring, flowering on successively produced young shoots from June to autumn, and a thoroughly good doer.

When I ask myself what I should specifically like the breeders to give us in the future, I would propose first, bright yellow, large-flowered clematis. Secondly, we could do with one or two more robust clematis of Jackmanii type, like Perle d'Azur but in deeper shades of blue, for late summer and autumn flowering. Ascotiensis is all we have in this line at the present.

4

Making the Most of Clematis

'Of course I should like a clematis, but I haven't the space; I just wouldn't know where to fit it in.' Nurserymen must have heard customers musing in this vein, time without number. Usually the old cliché: 'My garden's only the size of a pocket handkerchief' is thrown in for good measure. These remarks can mean one of two things: either that the gardener in question does not want to be tempted to buy a clematis anyway and is merely inventing reasons to bolster up his disinclination, or else that he really does believe what he is saying. While there is nothing anyone can do about altering the first state of mind, the second almost certainly arises from the misapprehension that a clematis needs a special place to itself. The reverse is, in fact, the case.

WALLS

Of all plants, clematis do *not* relish isolation. (For this reason, the notion of a clematis garden, as proposed by sundry author-enthusiasts, when swept away by their missionary zeal, has always struck me as ludicrously cracked.) They are sociable, flourishing on a modicum of competition; good mixers, enjoying the company of their neighbours. (Now and again they may happen to smother and kill one of these, but 'with no offence in the world'.) Most clematis lovers, however, tend to reserve special areas of wall space for their favourites. I am certainly not going to claim that this never works out successfully, but it does tend to emphasise the worst features of the clematis—an expanse of bare and far from shapely legs and, very often, a congested lump of blossom on top. If the clematis shoots had had a fairly bulky shrub like an evergreen ceanothus through which to thread their way, then their blossoms would have been distributed naturally and without overcrowding. In this way, too, the climber's own fundamental shapelessness would be wholly absorbed by the host shrub's structure, on which the clematis flowers would appear like jewels adorning a handsome woman's coiffure. So, my own reaction to a piece of bare wall space is to plant a shrub on it first and, when this has got a good lead in, say, two years' time, to follow on with a clematis.

It will be worth considering, at this point, which wall shrubs make good clematis supports, bearing in mind that almost any clematis will flourish on an east, south or west aspect, and a great many on a north wall, too. Climbing roses are superlative hosts—not that they possess any structural merit with which to mitigate the clematis's lack of it. Rather is it a case of each attempting to bury its defects in the other's embraces. When flowering, of course, both overflow with the vitality of high summer, and spill their bounty with an abandon that can transform the walls of even the tritest building, for a few weeks. Clematis and rose can be chosen either to give a succession of colour or else to flower simultaneously with the maximum impact. The climbing sports of bush hybrid tea and floribunda roses start to flower in late May just at the time when the large-flowered clematis which bloom on their old wood are also getting into their stride. From the pruning point of view these two types suit each other too, for in neither case is it necessary to be drastic and both can be dealt with together.

Clematis combine well with other climbing shrubs of greater vigour than their own and, in this context, wisteria is outstanding. Magnolias provide a good framework, but need several years' lead before the clematis is planted, and the same may be said of *Cotoneaster horizontalis* and *C. microphylla*. Pyracanthas, evergreen ceanothus and escallonias are robust wall plants which a clematis will much improve, while for a north aspect we have *Jasminum nudiflorum*, *Forsythia suspensa* and *Camellia japonica* hybrids.

If you have any wall fruit trees from which you despair of ever getting a decent crop—either because the fruit turns out not to be worth eating, or because the birds refuse to allow you any without a struggle that seems not worth making—then you should certainly drape them with clematis.

A natural gardener's reaction to the advice I have been giving here is: 'But won't it (the clematis) hurt my rose (forsythia, jasmine, fruit tree or whatever the supporter is going to be)?' And the answer is yes, probably it will, a little, but not enough to matter. This is a danger of which we should not be too frightened. After all, a satisfying garden is not made by growing every plant in it to perfection. That, rather, is the kind of treatment which vegetables should receive. A little competition between different types of plant will enable us to gain a far more pleasing result than if we grow all our treasures in evenly spaced blocks, beds and rows.

Back to our walls: there is one type of clematis which is sometimes invaluable for filling a large space, say two storeys high by 20 to 30 ft. across, and especially so on a rather dull, draughty north aspect. This is *C. montana* and its near relatives *C. chrysocoma*, *C.* × *vedrariensis* and *C. spoonerii*. They are too vigorous to be walled up with any other kind of plant, and can easily curtain the whole face, right down to the ground. But beware lest they get on to the roof and under the tiles, which they will lift recklessly. Of course, it is delightful to *see* a *montana* flung over a roof, especially someone else's roof.

Clematis will often be required to cover portions of free-standing garden walls, of every height and aspect, and there are one or two points worth noting, here. If the wall is a low one with its top below eye level, and the clematis is required to grow over and along the top, it will be best to plant it on the windward side, so that its shoots get blown in the required direction. Planted on the north side of a low wall, a clematis tends to get blown back off the top all the time, by prevailing south-westerlies. On the other hand, there is one axiom known to everyone with the slightest interest in growing clematis: that they like to have their roots in shade. If the south side of a wall cannot be made cool and shady at its base, it will often be possible to knock a brick out, low down, plant the clematis on the shady side and train its main stem through the hole. This is especially useful where high walls with their tops above eye level are concerned.

Artificial support must be provided for clematis grown straight on to walls, and this will be effected either with a wooden trellis or with wires. A fixing in the wall is best provided by vine-eye staples fastened into Rawlplugs. From these staples, stout galvanised iron wire is stretched both horizontally and vertically at 6 or 9 in. intervals. An easier method may be to fix pig-wire fencing (with a 6 in. square mesh) to the staples.

POLE, PERGOLA AND TRELLIS

One of the simplest ways to grow a clematis of medium vigour effectively is on a pole. This will usually be of chestnut, 10-12 ft. long, the bottom 3 ft. tarred, for long-lasting underground. Some gardeners like to give their clematis support by wrapping a sleeve of wire-netting round the pole, but I consider this unsightly, as parts of it are nearly always visible. I find the homely method of tying the clematis to its support with string at 6 in. intervals is perfectly effective and quite invisible. Tarred string should be used, as soft string or fillis will be attacked and plucked off by house sparrows for nesting material.

The kind of place to site a clematis on a pole will usually be as an isolated, vertical feature rising from a groundwork of lower-growing shrubs or herbaceous plants. Thus it is one of the finest adjuncts for inclusion in herbaceous, mixed or shrub borders of every kind. Sometimes it will be found that the entire weight of a clematis which is being grown over a shrub is too much for the latter. A pole strategically placed can be made to take three-parts of the burden, while a few strands of clematis are still allowed to wander over the shrub or other neighbouring plants.

Knowing how sensitive rose growers can be about the slightest encroachment on their darlings' territory by foreign bodies, I make my next suggestion with some diffidence, bowing to right and to left and retreating the while. Why not include a clematis or two on poles among your rose beds? The same rich soil conditions suit both shrubs ideally. I have found this practice especially successful among Hybrid Perpetual and Bourbon roses whose 6 to 8 ft. growths are being pegged down. You can tie the odd rose shoot to the pole, for a change, while the clematis will occasionally wander away among the pegged rose shoots. An ideal blending is thus achieved.

If you object to the starkness of your poles in winter, it is easy and practicable to remove them in autumn and restore them at, say, the end of March (the exact time depending on whether spring is early or late). But this works only where well-established clematis of the type that flower on the current season's young shoots are being grown. Such as these can be cut fairly hard back to 2 ft. or so, when the poles are being removed.

When a row of poles has been planted by way of a feature, then

8. Perle d'Azur. Light blue with pinkish-mauve flush.

9. Miss Bateman
(creamy-white)
trained on a fence.

10. Jackmanii alba.
White with pale
blue veins.

I would recommend associating clematis with climbing or rambler roses, rather than have them isolated. In this context, late-flowering clematis do combine especially well with rambler-type roses. It is only necessary to be prepared to delay the ramblers' pruning until autumn, rather than do it immediately after flowering, as tidy-minded rosarians will prefer. This should be no great hardship. The flowering of each will usually overlap, but the clematis is likely to reach its peak after the rose has spent itself. We are always recommended to grow rambler roses in an open situation where there is plenty of air movement, as this discourages powdery mildew from getting a hold on them. The same argument applies to Jackmanii and a number of other summer–autumn flowering clematis. Moreover, an anti-mildew spray will be as effective on the one as on the other.

Join a row of poles with wire and you have an open fence or trellis which, when planted up with roses, clematis, honeysuckles, vines and other climbers, will make an admirable screen, taking up far less space, in terms of thickness, than the average hedge. The temptation will be, however, to space the plants along it at equal distances, wheras as far as the clematis is concerned it will be better (unless there are plenty of low, ground-covering plants) to give it the protection of one of the other climbers which will help to shade its roots. The same treatment applies where clematis are being worked into a pergola of, say, roses or wisteria. And always plant the clematis on the shadier side of the rose, or what-ever it is. They need be no more than a foot or 18 in. apart.

TREES

The idea of growing a clematis over a tree is one which readily appeals, but you do want to know what you are doing, as there are a number of handy pitfalls.

If the tree is alive and flourishing, what chance has the clematis of battling with a creature so much larger and more overwhelming than itself? Any thought of planting a clematis with an oak or other forest tree should be dismissed out of hand. With crabs, ornamental cherries, any orchard tree, rowans, whitebeams and other trees of similarly moderate proportions, the prospects are brighter. But it is rather easy to forget, when planting near a deciduous tree in the dormant season, that its summer foliage will

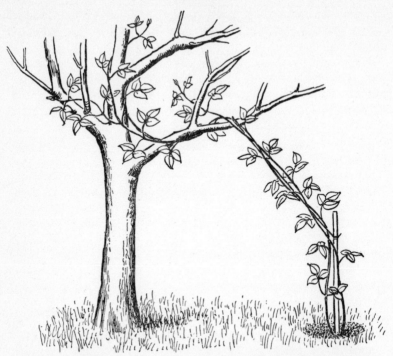

FIG. 1. GROWING CLEMATIS ON TREES. If a clematis is grown on a tree it has to compete with the latter for food, water and available light. A solution, when the branches of the tree come within 5 to 6 ft. of the ground, is to plant the clematis at the extremity of the branches and then lead it by a string to a selected branch. Where possible plant the clematis on the windward side, and if planting in turf keep a large circle around the plant clear of grass and heavily manured.

make life very trying for a plant beneath it which is struggling for light. Rowans do not cast too much shade, but cherries are especially umbrageous, while pears and whitebeams are little better. The trees' roots will also be competing for water and nutrients, so that the soil at the foot of a tree trunk is often as arid as a desert's. Here again trees vary; cherries are outstandingly greedy surface feeders while laburnum and the Judas tree (*Cercis siliquastrum*) tend to put their roots down rather than out. A sound rule of thumb, however, is to assume that a tree's roots will spread outwards at least as far as its branches. How slight are a clematis' chances when planted at the base of a tree trunk, is easily imagined.

The fact that the tree itself may be young and newly planted makes little difference. The same problem obtains but is deferred for a few years.

The solution which is feasible whenever the tree's lower branches reach reasonably close to the ground—within 5 or 6 ft., let us say— is to plant the clematis underneath a branch near its extremities, and then lead it up by a string to the branch itself. Where there is any choice in the matter, it will be wise to plant on the tree's windward side so that the clematis shoots are blown in the required direction.

Many gardeners fancy their tree adorned with the blossoms of a large-flowered clematis. Quite apart from the fact that in many situations and on many trees this would look inappropriate, the main consideration here is to choose a clematis which can cope with a tough situation. And the toughest clematis are all small flowered. But they are none the worse for that and, indeed, small trees offer a fine opportunity for growing a selection of clematis species and becoming acquainted with their great individuality and charm.

It should be added that, as trees are often grown in turf and therefore the clematis will be also, it has here yet another powerful competitor. However conscientious we are in keeping a large circle around the clematis clear of grass and heavily manured, we shall still need a robust grower.

When a clematis is required to deck a tree which is sickly, its prospects may be altogether more cheerful, with such greatly reduced competition for light, water and nutrients. I feel a bit Jeremiah-like in suggesting that here, too, a hidden danger may be lurking. Why is the tree sickly? And if the tree, why not the clematis also? Mr Basil Furneaux once asked me why an apple tree in my Long Border was dying. 'Old age,' said I, glibly. He shook his head, and intimated that there was no such cause. As any fruit grower will have guessed before I say it, the tree was being killed by the parasitic Honey Fungus (*Armillaria mellea*). This does not confine its attentions to fruit trees. It is practically omnivorous, and if one were to plant a clematis against an infected tree, the former might die of the same cause. And, naturally, the same argument applies to other possible causes of the tree's ill health. It might, for instance, have been starved in some way or else waterlogged.

Still, there is no point in worrying oneself sick by proxy, and it will probably be best to plant the clematis anyway, giving it as generous a start as may be, and thereafter simply keep one's eyes open for trouble so that it can be nipped in the bud if possible. Dead trees should be regarded with the same wariness. They can be an excellent medium for displaying clematis and other climbers but should not be regarded as permanent fixtures. The more you cover them, the more leverage they offer to the wind. Their top-hamper of smaller branches should be considerably reduced at the start, and if the main trunk does not offer a clematis sufficient anchorage, some strands of wire can be discreetly added as they are required.

SHRUBS

Of all the practicable and attractive ways in which clematis may be exploited, their association with shrubs offers the greatest scope. Yet to most gardeners this is still an untrodden path. It is only a matter of getting into the right frame of mind. Every mature shrub of reasonable proportions should be regarded from time to time with a questioning: 'How would you look with a clematis growing over you?' Examples of a few that I have found especially suitable hosts are: brooms (especially *Spartium*), cotoneasters, tree paeonies (species), shrub roses, viburnums, berberis, *Hibiscus syriacus*, escallonias, lilacs, *Senecio laxifolius* and spiraeas.

Shrubs of stiff habit make better supports than those which are whippy and blow about in the wind a lot. It is difficult for a clematis to make initial contact with a plant which will never keep still. One can plant quite close up to a shrub like a rose or a broom, but when it has a greedy, fibrous, surface-feeding root system, like a lilac or a hibiscus, the clematis must be planted well out—perhaps as much as 6 ft. from the shrub's base, and then led on to its branches. Again, as for trees, plant on the windward side whenever you can.

TREE STUMPS AND GROUND COVER

I am concerned, in this chapter, to discuss how clematis may be used and to leave consideration of the actual varieties best suited

11. Jackmanii rubra. Velvety crimson-lake.

12. Nelly Moser. Rosy-mauve with carmine bar.

for special purposes to a chapter of its own. Suffice it to say here, then, that certain clematis are good ground coverers, but with the reservation that, being deciduous, they are not properly covering the ground the whole time. The happiest solution is to grow them *among* evergreen ground coverers. Thus, an occasional clematis rambling over a groundwork of dwarf heathers (whether summer or winter flowering) is very effective indeed.

Large trees, when cut down, often leave a stump perhaps a foot high which is difficult to get rid of. A clematis will do the trick of concealment, but it is nearly always necessary to fix a piece of wire-netting over the top of the stump first.

ORNAMENTAL TUBS, POTS AND ALI BABA JARS

There is a strong demand for clematis that will enjoy being grown in tubs, pots, urns and the like. Many old country cottages, converted to a higher standard of living, have been made damp-proof only at the expense of a wide concrete footing all round their base, which precludes the planting of wall shrubs and climbers in the ground. The only possible alternative is to grow them in large tubs. Then again the patios of many a town dwelling give little or no scope for planting except in tubs and pots and, indeed, these can often be of such pleasing appearance in themselves that they lend an air to any garden.

In such circumstances, a clematis will be required to grow either up a wall, from the container, or else to flop out of and entwine the container itself—a procedure which is especially effective when the tall Ali Baba-type jar is being used. A great many clematis varieties will meet these requirements if they are given extra-specially generous and solicitous cultural treatment. It is, after all, not very pleasant to have your roots cooped up in a pot for life. The strongest (John Innes No. 3) potting compost needs to be used with additional liquid feeds during the growing season; the largest available container should be chosen so as to allow as much root room as possible, and the container must never be allowed to dry out. It must, of course have a drainage hole at the bottom. If, after four or five years, the clematis seems to be doing not so well, I should turn it out in the dormant season and completely replace all its soil with a fresh batch.

C

As clematis hate to be hot at the roots, they will be happier with other plants in the same container. For the same reason an east or west aspect will try them less than a south, while for those varieties which will flower freely near or against a north wall (see page 57), this position will be better than any.

5

On Choosing Clematis

(1) FOR SIZE, COLOUR AND SPECTACLE

The last chapter was concerned with reviewing the uses to which clematis can be applied in the garden, without going into details of varieties. But some sort of a critical survey of the different types and varieties available for various purposes must surely be helpful. In this, the first of two chapters on the subject, I shall assume that the gardener wants to make a splash with a large-flowered hybrid, and that if I can advise him on what to look for in the colour range that interests him, he can find in his garden a suitable place for what sounds good. Many clematis will necessarily be left out of this survey, which will be unfair, I admit, and does not necessarily mean that they are not worth considering. It probably means that I do not know them well enough to feel entitled to discuss them. That is the trouble with writing a specialist book before one is at least an octogenarian. Another unfairness is that my opinion is just my opinion and there is nothing absolute about a very personal appraisal.

'BLUE' CLEMATIS

Ascotiensis
Beauty of Worcester
Blue Gem
Durandii
Elsa Späth
Etoile de Paris
Hybrida Sieboldii (Ramona)
Lady Northcliffe
Lasurstern

Lord Nevill
Mrs Bush
Mrs Cholmondeley
Mrs Hope
Mrs P. B. Truax
Perle d'Azur
Prins Hendrik (Prince Henry)
William Kennett

We have already admitted that the colouring of no clematis comes near to pure blue, yet we continue to speak of blue clematis. The cynic will say that this is a nurseryman's gambit, as blue is the best selling colour of all. Rather is it a matter of comparison, I think. There are so many clematis which come indisputably into the mauve-lavender-lilac bracket, that when they do verge on blue we might just as well call them this. I would say that it was the most exciting colour among clematis, and that the demand for a big blue one was the greatest of any, while deep blues tend to be more popular than the lighter shades.

In the deep blue category, then, the choice lies between four excellent varieties. Lasurstern has already been adequately praised (p. 11). Lady Northcliffe is every bit as good, the flower most beautifully shaped, but I have myself been unlucky in establishing this variety, and it has frequently gone down to 'wilt'. These two have a white 'eye'; in Lord Nevill it is purple, in a bold flower of great substance and a plant of good constitution. Beauty of Worcester has double flowers with a white eye, in early summer, and well-formed single blooms on the young shoots later on. It is a first-class clematis. The other three also carry two crops if they are growing strongly, but the first flush tends to be the heavier.

Among the lighter blue shades and again with a double flowering season, my first choice would be Mrs Hope—an enormous bloom at its first appearance with such smoothness of texture that one wants to stroke it, and a handsome boss of purple stamens. Of a rather similar texture and size but slightly deeper colouring is Elsa Späth, while the old favourite William Kennett is similarly coloured but of an unusually rough texture. Moore and Jackman's comment of ninety years ago was that it is 'wanting in refinement', but the fact remains that it has triumphed over time and is a showy, good-tempered clematis. A number of varieties very similar to Mrs Hope are terribly jumbled up in nursery collections, so that in ordering one you are just as likely to get one of the others, namely: Hybrida Sieboldii (synonymous with 'Ramona,' a popular American cultivar), Blue Gem, Sensation, Mrs Bush and William Kennett.

Were one judging the flower alone, Prins Hendrik (*syn.* Prince Henry) would head the list of paler blue varieties as its outsize blooms consist of magnificent, broad, overlapping sepals, wavy margined and altogether delectable, but this is a notoriously difficult clematis to get established.

13. Marcel Moser. Rosy-mauve with carmine central bar.

14. President (light purple) growing on *Spiraea arguta* in a mixed border.

Mrs P. B. Truax, always described as 'periwinkle blue', is quite pretty and easy to grow, but after flowering profusely in May and June is disinclined for any further effort. Mrs Cholmondeley, by contrast, is just about the most prolific of all the large-flowered hybrids, blooming almost continuously from May till autumn. At the onset of its great spate, the flowers are 8 in. across but look less, as the (usually) six sepals are very narrow with large gaps between them towards the base. The colour is palish lavender-blue and its main value is in the massed effect. In Etoile de Paris, the star-shaped flower with pointed sepals is a little gappy but stiff and firm of texture: a good mauve-blue with reddish central bars that disappear on fading.

So far we have considered only those varieties which start by flowering on their old wood. Turning to those which are usually hard pruned and flower on their young shoots from late June till early September, Perle d'Azur is outstanding. It is very near Jackmanii in the shape and plantain-like grooving of its sepals, and of a light, showy blue rather more mauve towards the centre. It is vigorous and, really, Ascotiensis is no less so with a much deeper blue colouring and pointed sepals. Though their individual flowers are nothing out of the ordinary, there are no other blue clematis in late summer which can serve us with quite the bounty of these two.

The last blue clematis up for discussion is in a different class from all the rest. Durandii resulted from a cross between Jackmanii and the herbaceous non-climbing species, *C. integrifolia*. It is non-climbing and almost herbaceous itself. Growing to about 8 ft. in a season, one can either let it flop over neighbouring shrubs or tie it to a post. The flowers are borne from midsummer onwards and are 4 in. across, of an intense indigo-blue with a white eye. Durandii can get 'wilt' but it is a good doer by and large. It is a fine and unique looking clematis.

WHITE CLEMATIS

Duchess of Edinburgh
Henryi (syn. Bangholme
   Belle)
Huldine
Jackmanii alba

Lucie Lemoine
Marie Boisselot
   (syn. Mme Le Coultre)
Miss Bateman
Mrs George Jackman

The large white clematis are possessed of such shining splendour that, seen in a garden, the viewer stops in his tracks; and when glimpsed at the roadside, a vehicle driver will be in danger of an accident. Their impact is, indeed, terrific. Even those who mulishly refuse to countenance white flowers, may experience rebellious stirrings when confronted by one of these.

I have no hesitation in awarding highest marks, here, to Marie Boisselot. Unfortunately she is just as often encountered in the catalogues as Mme Le Coultre, and so I was fooled into buying her twice. It is usually a healthy variety of unbounded vigour, making fresh growth from April till August. An established specimen never fails to carry two enormous crops of blossoms which are 7 in. across in the first, early summer series. The timing of the second batch varies a good deal with the heat of the season; it starts in August or September and continues, frosts permitting, into November. The flowers are very full and well shaped, white throughout, including the stamens. Mrs George Jackman is slightly darker centred; its blooms are of classic outline. It is not quite so vigorous.

Miss Bateman has medium vigour too, and its cushion of dark, purplish anthers is a special attraction. Other things being equal, a pale flower with a dark eye is preferable to one which is pale throughout. Henryi is another large white clematis with a dark eye and a long flowering season—a great favourite with those whom it has favoured, of which happy band I, alas, am not one. It never stops 'wilting' for me and, I can fairly add, for many another.

Duchess of Edinburgh and Lucie Lemoine are another couple in which I can detect no difference. They carry medium-large, double flowers. At their best they are quite pleasing, but only too often they are deformed and largely green so that it appears as though they could not make up their minds whether to be leaves or flowers. Thus they will appeal to flower arrangers for ever on the search for something different. Their constitution tends to be weakly and they seldom flower a second time. Jackmanii alba is a very different kettle of fish. It always flowers twice and the first crop is semi-double, consisting of sepals whose size and shape varies a good deal, producing a ragged effect. Their colour is white with blue veins, redolent of skimmed milk. The second crop is larger and composed of nicely shaped single blooms of moderate size. A rampant grower, this, with very pale green foliage.

Finally Huldine, for which I have a great affection. Huldine (a German diminutive for Hilda) is vigorous and reliable so long as it gets plenty of sun; otherwise it may run to leaf. It blooms from July onwards and the flowers are only 4 in. across, of a most distinctive shape. Given flat lighting, the flowers are white, but back lighting reveals the sepals' mauvish undersides in a pearly translucence. They are excellent for cutting.

'RED' CLEMATIS

Crimson King	Mme Edouard André
Duchess of Sutherland	Mme Grangé
Ernest Markham	Mme Jules Corrévon
Jackmanii rubra	Ville de Lyon

None of the red clematis is either true red or orange-red; they all have more or less of blue in their colouring. They also tend to be only medium-large in their blooms—not nearly as big as many of the paler coloured cultivars.

Perhaps the largest (if we exclude Barbara Dibley, which I have put in the Nelly Moser section) and certainly the most beautiful in colouring and shape is Duchess of Sutherland. Its colouring of intense carmine red is bright and effective without being crude, while its six finely tapering sepals compose a well-formed flower. From old wood in early summer it will carry some very attractive double blooms of rather flattened form, but its main contribution of single blooms comes in late summer. Its vigour is sometimes only moderate and it is not always easy to establish. Unfortunately there are 'two competing forms of Duchess of Sutherland moving in and out of nurseries in the oddest fashion,' as my exceedingly well-informed correspondent Mr Chave, of Vancouver, aptly puts it. The form I have described is the one I know and grow. The other, which conforms more closely to the traditional description of this variety, has a decidedly whitened area down the mid-rib of the sepals and these are not markedly pointed.

Crimson King, with a slightly smaller flower but equally intense colouring, is again sometimes tricky to get going. Ernest Markham, on the other hand, is robust—so much so that unless grown in a really sunny position it sometimes runs entirely to leaf. It will flower twice, more heavily the second time. Its blooms are bold if a little coarse, with six broad sepals, recurved towards their blunt tips, in colour a good magenta (not too much blue in it)—a showy variety, in fact, when it obliges by flowering for you.

Ville de Lyon is dependably one of the freest flowering of all large-flowered hybrids and, doubtless for this reason, the most widely grown. It flowers in two big flushes from the end of May, and with the briefest interval between them, right through to September. The blooms, of moderate size, are well held on long, stiff stems, and there is something about their rounded shape which is thoroughly satisfying. Their two-toned colouring is an interesting feature since the margin of the sepals is a bright carmine shade while the inner area is paler. If there is a fault to find it is that this inner area has a slightly muddy hue, like strawberries when they have gone off. The stamens make a nice bright cream cushion, in contrast to the other varieties so far described, whose stamens are a dirty yellowish-brown.

Another good red with especially pleasing crimson lake colouring is Jackmanii rubra. It blooms twice, very freely, with double flowers of slightly unbalanced shape on the first occasion. And it grows well. So does Mme Jules Corrévon, with one big crop from the end of June. Its twisted sepals have an air of informality which makes a welcome change. It is a nice bright rosy-red and very free. Mme Edouard André is by no means difficult, but its general appearance is 'petite'—the very antithesis of Ernest Markham. The flowers of Mme Edouard André have rather pointed sepals and in colouring are deep and vinous. It should always be grown where the maximum of sunshine can bring out its colouring, and yet, even then, it has a matt-ness, a deficiency in highlights which gives this popular variety a certain lifelessness in my eyes.

Mme Grangé is darker still; so dark as really to demand a white background such as weather-boarding or whitewash or paint. Yet it is of a truly sumptuous and velvety texture; I like this variety. It is very vigorous and flowers in July and August on its young shoots. Sometimes a severe winter will cut it hard back to ground level.

NELLY-MOSER-TYPE CLEMATIS

Barbara Dibley	Lincoln Star
Barbara Jackman	Marcel Moser

Bees' Jubilee   Mrs N. Thompson
Bracebridge Star   Nelly Moser
King George V   Sealand Gem

Next to Jackmanii, Nelly Moser is the most popular of all the large-flowered cultivars. It has a strikingly individual appearance, with that vivid carmine bar running down the centre of each mauve sepal, and as this character and the general shape of the flower are shared by a number of varieties, I shall consider them as a group. They all have a marked tendency to fading in strong sunlight, and in particular the central bar. It is for this reason that they are recommended for planting on north walls, and not because they are happier in this aspect than elsewhere or than other large-flowered clematis.

Nelly Moser has eight rather blunt-tipped sepals which make its outline circular rather than star-shaped. Add to this the spoke-like effect of its bars, and the whole flower looks remarkably wheel-like with a boss of handsome purplish stamens for a hub. The blooms are some $6\frac{1}{2}$ in. across and produced with great freedom in May and June. If the plant is growing strongly, it will carry a second crop in autumn and this tends to be more brightly coloured than the first. Indeed, I have known November blooms to be brilliant carmine all over. The jolly harlequin get-up of Nelly Moser is frowned on by some who like their colours straight, but it is good tempered and showy and carries its blooms well.

Marcel Moser, which came out in 1896, a year before Nelly Moser, is not so vigorous and needs the best of growing conditions. Its flowers are similarly coloured but larger and handsomer with finely pointed sepals. King George V and Bees' Jubilee both have very bright colouring of the same type, but the latter is a prime 'wilter' and difficult to establish, while the former, although having the useful attribute of carrying its main crop after mid-summer, is reputed to be shy flowering. Sealand Gem is pale lilac with a darker bar and makes a good show, although the blooms are individually undistinguished.

Lincoln Star is a gem, with only medium-sized flowers consisting of eight narrow, pointed sepals overlapping at the base, of a brilliant raspberry pinky-red throughout. And the stamens are the same colour but rather darker. Unfortunately it is not a strong grower. Neither is Bracebridge Star, and this variety, though comparable with the last, is of more gappy form and less striking colouring.

Barbara Jackman is a remarkable clematis. Its flowers are fully open while still 3 to 4 in. across and continue to enlarge thereafter to $5\frac{1}{2}$ in. At the first stage they are vivid bluish-purple with a magenta central bar. As they grow they fade to greyish-mauve and the central bar becomes a tired purplish-red. Although my description may not make it sound so, Barbara Jackman is pleasing at both ends of its flowering and I like to see a plant hung with blooms at every stage of their development. I do not regard them as any the worse for being exposed to sunlight. It is otherwise with Barbara Dibley, whose 6-in. flowers open a gloriously vivacious petunia-red throughout, but fade to dust and ashes. My first sight of this clematis was against an aggressively red brick wall. Imagine! These last two varieties are quite easy to please. The recently introduced Mrs N. Thompson is striking on the show bench and resembles a very dark Barbara Jackman with petunia-red central bars and bluish-purple margins. I have no experience of it in the garden.

PURPLE CLEMATIS

Daniel Deronda	Lady Betty Balfour
Gipsy Queen	President
Guiding Star	Star of India
Jackmanii	Victoria
Jackmanii superba	

There are some fine varieties here and none that I should like to be without, except for Jackmanii itself which is outclassed by Jackmanii superba. A feature common to all of them, except for Victoria, is that their blooms open reddish-purple and fade to bluish-purple.

It was the gaps between its sepals that gave Jackmanii a thin appearance and let it down. Jackmanii superba has a fuller flower with broad sepals, four, five or six in number. It is very vigorous and carries vast quantities of bloom for six to eight weeks from the end of June. So much unrelieved purple can be oppressively stuffy and the great thing with this clematis is to break its monotony with other flowers—the bright yellow of many giant mulleins, for instance, the lambent torches of the big kniphofias and the creamy plumes of *Artemisia lactiflora*. I prefer to site Jackmanii superba in a border of sorts for this reason, and also because it often mildews badly against a house. Victoria is in every way similar except for its colouring, which is infinitely more pleasing. The flowers open a light rosy-purple and gradually fade to a nice deep mauve.

In colouring, Gipsy Queen is similar to Jackmanii superba and also in its manner of flowering on young shoots of the current season, but in shape its flowers are quite different and much prettier, with six finely tapered sepals and a boss of dark stamens. Star of India differs from Jackmanii superba in only two respects: it is not so vigorous, but it has a broad velvety reddish band down the centre of each sepal, which makes it altogether more interesting. Lady Betty Balfour, the last in this group to flower entirely on young shoots, opens its season in late August. It makes swags of growth each year and the six nicely tapered sepals of its quite large blooms are offset by whitish stamens. It must have full sun, else it may fail to bloom, and even then it sometimes mysteriously does not make buds. I suspect that damage by capsids to the growing points, at just that time in July-August when buds should be developing, may be the cause.

The next three varieties all start to bloom in May. The 6-in. flowers of Guiding Star are truly star-like with six fine-pointed sepals which taper at each end and have large, but evenly spaced, gaps between them. It is a sprightly flower. The colour is bluish-purple with reddish-purple streaks scattered here and there.

President (often called The President) is one of the best clematis ever and deserves my expatiation. Except in the coldest summers, and as long as it is kept growing strongly, it will flower three times annually: in May-June on old wood; in July, and again in September-October on young shoots, On their first appearance the flowers are 7 in. across, but only some 5 in. later. They are somewhat cupped and, being held upright, one is delightedly conscious of their silvery undersurface, which contrasts strongly with the uniformly rich blue-purple of the upper surface. Why some descriptions should ascribe a paler bar down the centre of each sepal's upper surface, I cannot imagine, as this feature belongs to Daniel Deronda and is one of its main distinguishing characters from

President. The latter has dark reddish-purple stamens and deeply bronzed young foliage—altogether a winner.

Daniel Deronda, then, is of much the same colouring but always wears a whitened area near the midrib on its top side. At its first appearance in May, the blooms are large and double, of the flattened rather than the domed type. Later crops come single.

PINK, FLESH, MAUVE AND GREY CLEMATIS

Beauty of Richmond	Lady Caroline Nevill
Belle Nantaise	Lady Londesborough
Belle of Woking	Mme Baron-Veillard
Comtesse de Bouchaud	Miss Crawshay
Countess of Lovelace	Mrs Spencer Castle
Edouard Desfossé	Percy Picton
Fair Rosamond	Proteus
Fairy Queen	Vyvyan Pennell
Hagley Hybrid	W. E. Gladstone

Rather an omnibus group, this, but scarcely worth further subdivision. I will start with clematis that can reasonably pass for pink, graduate to the deep lilac and mauve shades, and then watch them growing ever paler till we are almost back at white.

If we could draw on clematis of the clear shades of pink that we see illustrated in nurserymen's catalogues, we should indeed be fortunate. The cold light of reality reveals, however, that they are all tainted with mauve. The best is Hagley Hybrid, a warm rosy-mauve variety without a vestige of harshness in its colouring. Its six pointed sepals tend to be boat shaped, with inrolled margins, and the dark, purplish anthers are a telling feature. It starts flowering in late June, sometimes earlier, and continues well into September. Hagley Hybrid is not exempt from 'wilt' but, by and large, it is a thoroughly good doer. So is Comtesse de Bouchaud, another bright pinkish clematis but of far cruder colouring, with a good deal of blue on its palette. Nevertheless, it is a very good clematis. The flowers start to appear on young shoots about mid-June, and the remainder open in one huge flush over the next two months. My own plant covers some 22 ft. of an 8 ft. wall and is a curtain of blossom. Its season ends just as Mme Baron-Veillard's begins—in August. The latter is every bit as vigorous. Its lilac-rose

15. Jackmanii superba (purple with reddish tinge) on a pole in a mixed border.

16. Countess of Lovelace. Lilac-blue.

flowers are deeper toned than those of the Countess, with more pointed sepals, but bluer than Hagley Hybrid. A bungalow I often pass near Hastings has it associated unexpectedly but effectively with Lasurstern. The latter is hard pruned annually and hence concentrates all its flowering on to its young growth, thus coinciding with its neighbour.

Mrs Spencer Castle and Miss Crawshay are both pale pink shaded with lilac and semi-double at their first flowering in May and June. The latter only makes the one effort with me, but Mrs Spencer Castle continues with single blooms. Which brings me to Proteus, whose first crop of dome-shaped blooms have more sepals packed into them than any clematis I know. Gross, you might think, but in fact they are as well formed as a double opium poppy. Their colour is an unusual and, to me, very attractive dull pinkish-lilac. Later blooms are single. Vyvyan Pennell is essentially deep lilac without the reddish tinge of Proteus. It is an even better shape, for the broad outer sepals stand out from and frame the inner, lavender-blue rosette. Again, it comes single later. For anyone wanting to try a large double clematis for the first time, I would recommend this variety on account of its vigour.

In the deep mauve category that we have now reached, Edouard Desfossé carries outsize blooms with reddish central bars and carmine anthers, borne in early summer on a vigorous plant. I am not sure that I care about its colouring. Percy Picton, of a pure and intense mauve with a dark eye, is distinctly weak growing and prone to 'wilt'.

And so to the rich lavender W. E. Gladstone. A real aristocrat, this, despite its name. The flowers are enormous and—a rare feature among the largest-flowered clematis—they are carried on young shoots from early July till autumn. Like Mrs Hope, they are of satin-smooth texture but more floppy. The dark anthers contrast handsomely. W. E. Gladstone carries a sprinkling of blossoms over a long period, but could never be described as free. In some winters it gets cut to the ground. Indeed, there was one year when my plant did not reappear until June, but I have never had it killed. William Kennett is sometimes sold in its stead. After all, they both begin with 'W'.

Countess of Lovelace is a beauty if you can get it going, but young plants tend to be weakly so you should accept only the best. Its double pompoms are bluish-lilac with a small green eye, and as it fades a good deal, a fairly shaded position is the best. In Belle Nantaise we have a large, pale lavender flower with long, pointed sepals and cream stamens. Like W. E. Gladstone, it flowers on its young shoots from July to October but is far more prolific. I decided to move my plant when it was over twenty years old, and I was forgiven.

Beauty of Richmond and Lady Caroline Nevill are rather similar with large, pale bluish-mauve flowers, fading to grey, and, in the case of the latter variety, often semi-double at first. Beauty of Richmond starts a deeper colour and has cream stamens whereas in Lady Caroline the stamens are brown tipped. I would not look twice at either of them if Lady Londesborough were around. The shape of its flower is exquisite with seven, round, broadly overlapping sepals. They open pale mauve, fade to silvery-mauve and are forcefully offset by dark stamens with reddish-purple anthers. It flowers, mainly, in early summer, and so does Belle of Woking whose colouring might again be described as silvery-mauve but whose shape is in absolute contrast to that of Lady Londesborough, being fully double in globular form. Its flowers last for ages, as is so often the way when they are double.

Finally, two very pale flesh-coloured clematis. Fairy Queen bears flowers of the largest size in early summer and, with their dark eyes, they are certainly effective. The blooms are smaller but more regular in Fair Rosamond, a white background being overlaid with pink reticulation. The stamens are rich purple. It is a charming old variety and scented.

6

On Choosing Clematis

(2) FOR SPECIAL PURPOSES

As some clematis are useful for more than one special purpose, there is inevitably a good deal of overlapping of material in this chapter. While the large-flowered hybrids must come into the picture at times, it is the small-flowered species and hybrids to which I particularly want to turn our critical attention here. It is a mistake to think of them as either superior or inferior to their large-flowered cousins. Some are relatively inconspicuous but others are very gay. There is, however, a great difference of impact between a sheet of colour composed of small units and a sheet composed of large. The former will tend to look most appropriate when casting its tresses over the wilder features of a garden, while the latter will be pleased to vie with all that is flamboyant in the most highly sophisticated areas of the flower garden.

TO COVER TREES, GARAGES AND
LARGE AREAS OF BUILDINGS

It sometimes causes disappointment that the number of clematis suitable for these purposes is so restricted and that by far and away the most effective are *C. montana* and its near relatives, already so familiar to us all. However, there are slight variations within this theme, so let us take a closer look at the group. *C. montana* itself has white flowers like the sails of a windmill; its four sepals are narrow with wide gaps between them. It smells strongly of vanilla and can be detected at a considerable distance from the plant especially, of course, in warm May weather and when the plant is in a sunny position. *C. montana rubens* is the pinky-mauve form, which varies enough in size and intensity of colouring to have collected a large number of varietal names, e.g., Elizabeth, Tetrarose, Pink Perfection, Picton's Variety. I would hesitate to choose between them. All that matters is that they should not be washed out in colouring and that they should have retained the characteristic vanilla scent.

Clematis montana grandiflora is a larger flowered and even more vigorous form of the species, with white blossoms on long stems but no scent. Curiously, it takes two or three years for a young plant to settle down to the business of flowering. *C. montana wilsonii*, again white, has the distinction of flowering a month later than its brethren, i.e., in June and July, but if you are unlucky in your purchase, as I have been, you will find it flowering at exactly the same time as the ordinary *montana*.

Clematis chrysocoma is like a superior version of *C. montana rubens*, except in lacking scent. Its leaves are handsomely cut, bronzed when young and covered with a down of soft short hairs. Its sepals are broader than those of *montana* so that the flower is of rounder appearance and borne on an extra-long stalk. This species has the welcome habit of carrying a quite generous aftermath of blossom on its young shoots in late summer and autumn. Crossed with *C. montana rubens*, it gave rise to the hybrid *C. ×* *vedrariensis* (sometimes confusingly known as *spoonerii rosea*), which has very large flowers, when correctly named. A form of it called Highdown Variety is claimed to be an improvement, and with such a name it should be. Finally there is *C. spoonerii*, said by some to be a distinct species though also known as *C. chrysocoma sericea*, with downy leaves and stems and 3-in. white flowers on long petioles.

Next in vigour to the *montana* series I should place *C. rehderiana* (syn. *C. nutans*). Although by no means showy, it has two valuable attributes in its late flowering (August-October) and a deliciously powerful cowslip scent. Its coarsely toothed and much divided foliage is inclined to mask the axillary panicles of small, bell-shaped flowers which are the dingy colour of straw (not primrose-yellow, as the catalogues would have us believe). It will climb 20 ft. into a tree.

While the hawthorn scented *C. paniculata* and our native *C. vitalba* would both do their cloaking task quite well, the former flowers too late in autumn in our climate while the latter is scarcely of sufficient interest to be planted in the garden until one has run

1. Barbara Dibley on an espalier-trained pear

2. An example of the difficulty of nomenclature. Sold as the variety Perle d'Azur, the shape, in the author's view is correct for Lady Northcliffe, but the colour for Mrs. P. B. Truax

3. *C. florida bicolor* with the rose Paul's Scarlet Climber

out of other ideas such as *Vitis coignetiae, Wisteria* and the ultra-vigorous types of climbing roses.

TO COVER SMALL TREES AND LARGE SHRUBS

So far as covering shrubs is concerned, most of the large-flowered hybrids will serve our purpose. Some of the small-flowered species and hybrids demand consideration here, however, as they are easy, trouble free (none of them suffer from 'wilt'), tremendously free flowering and they look comfortably at home when swathing the branches of a tree, whereas in similar circumstances a large-flowered type could look self-conscious. I remember pronouncing to a certain clematis lover who wished to enlarge her collection, that I considered a variety like Lasurstern would probably not flourish in her light, drought-prone soil. 'Oh! but I have established it, and it's doing very well,' she said, leading me to the spot. There, indeed, was Lasurstern, in full flower on a twisted old apple tree. 'The trouble is, I don't think I like it there,' she went on. 'What shall I do?' Indeed, it did look odd.

First, then, *C. viticella* and its closely related hybrids. They all flower after midsummer on young wood and can be cut back more or less hard annually, according to how much space they are required to cover. They will climb up to 12 or 15 ft. if necessary. Their flowers are 2 or 3 in. across and usually nod on bent pedicels. *C. viticella* is itself worth growing; so prolific when in flower that its foliage is scarcely noticeable. It is a medium-toned, rather dusky purple. *Viticella rubra* is a deep and glowing red with the minimum of pink mixed into it—a wonderful sight when the sun shines through its sepals. It has often been sold as Royal Velours and also as Kermesina. The former has larger flowers of a royal purple but the latter is something of a mystery to me and I am not certain whether I have ever seen the real thing. It should be a wine-red of sorts. Another variety which frequently masquerades as Kermesina is Margot Koster. The latter is distinctly rosy-red with flowers that are not markedly pendant and somewhat larger than the average *viticella*. They consist of four, five or six sepals and these become reflexed at the tips and the margins, so that the overall shape is nothing much, but, what with a lively colour and vast quantities of blossom, this is certainly a good clematis.

A particular favourite with me is Abundance, which resembles

D

C. viticella in all respects except for colour: this is 'vin rosé', but rather redder towards the centre of the sepal and bluer towards the margin. Its network of veins stands out because a deeper red than the rest of the flower. And the plant is well-named. In Minuet we find a white flower with mauve veins and margins—altogether too indeterminate as though its colours had run in the wash. Little Nell is rather similar, its white central band shading to mauve at the margins. A small flower (Nell's are 3 in. across) needs to have a more definite colouring if it is to create an impression. Alba luxurians is rather a pet, though; its pure white flowers shade to green at the tips. This may sound a bit fey, but when carefully placed against a dark background it is a sweetie.

The next two, though still obviously close to *C. viticella*, have rather larger flowers (about 4 in. across) held upright, instead of nodding, and opening quite flat. Indeed, in Etoile Violette the six sepals recurve at their tips. In colouring this clematis is the very dark purple of Jackmanii but is relieved by its cream eye of stamens. Venosa Violacea has five or six boat-shaped sepals. They are purple at the margins and white in the centre, but this central area is overlaid with a network of purple veins. This is a fascinating clematis to look into.

Clematis campaniflora is a Portuguese species, nearly related to *C. viticella*. Its slender, spidery shoots are hung with rather broadly campanulate bells, about an inch across at the mouth, in late summer. They are the colour of skimmed milk, but have their own discreet brand of charm.

Another group which is especially useful for providing a light mantle over shrubs is the *texensis* hybrids (see Chapter 3, p. 23). They are not unduly leafy and hence their smothering effect has been reduced to a minimum. At least three varieties—Grace Darling, Duchess of York and Admiration—seem to have fallen out of cultivation, but if any reader knows of a plant of one or other of these, I should be grateful to be informed of it, with a view to bringing it back into circulation. Of those which are still available, Gravetye Beauty differs from the rest in that its four or five sepals open wide into a gappy, star-shaped flower, $2\frac{1}{2}$ to 3 in. across. It looks its best when half opened and still bell shaped, the colour being a magnificent ruby-red. The remainder keep their lily-flowered tulip shape throughout the flower's life, their season extending from July to October. Gravetye Beauty dies down right to the ground annually but will climb a good 10 ft. from scratch. Countess of Onslow is rather woodier and will go up to 15 ft. if required to. The flowers are borne singly from the leaf axils in the last 2 ft. of growth. Their four sepals each consist of a rather thick central zone of a deep cherry-red, surrounded by a thinner textured margin of a warm but pale pink. It looks especially pretty when associated with the autumn blossoms of one of the evergreen ceanothus such as A. T. Johnson or Autumnal Blue, with pure blue flowers.

Duchess of Albany is the clearest shade of pink in any clematis I know; bright and thoroughly effective. Etoile Rose is somewhere between the last two in colouring, distinctly mauver than Duchess of Albany, but very pretty. Sir Trevor Lawrence, of a deep carmine, is showy and eye catching. These *texensis* hybrids only need to be seen growing in gardens to win easy and deserved popularity.

Clematis tangutica and *C. orientalis* are both well suited to covering small trees and large shrubs. These are the two species of bright yellow-flowered clematis which are most commonly grown. Those who do not know them in the flesh are liable to get an inflated conception of their size from descriptions and from close-up coloured photographs in which the scale is not apparent. Once the fact has been accepted that their sepals are seldom more than $1\frac{1}{2}$ in. long, it is easy to appreciate the many good qualities in these two. They start flowering in late June and continue till October, long before which time the plants are covered with a fuzz of ripening seed heads. Three selections of *C. tangutica* are on the market: *obtusiuscula* and Gravetye Variety have no marked advantage over the result of sowing a pinch of seed from any decent-looking plant. Jack Drake's form, however, is more than twice their size. With *C. orientalis* it is essential to get hold of the form collected by Ludlow and Sherriff in Tibet and still known by its collector's number L. and S. 13342. Its finely dissected foliage is a good feature in itself, while the broadly campanulate flowers are shaped like cow-bells, and consist of four very thick segments inevitably reminding one of lemon peel. Their colour is bright ochreous yellow while the anthers are dark. It is the most cheerful looking climbing plant imaginable.

Clematis flammula makes a good deal of heavy growth in a season and therefore needs a fairly tough supporting shrub. Its foliage is an unusually deep green, but completely obliterated at flowering time in late summer and autumn, by the myriads of tiny white, heavily scented blossoms. Crossed with *C. viticella*, this has produced *C.* × *rubro-marginata*—and a worthless, dirty-looking product it is, in my view, with flowers not a bit rubro but white, edged with dim purple.

FOR HERBACEOUS BORDERS

Any clematis can be grown in a herbaceous border on a tripod or single pole, but some are especially suitable in this milieu. *C. recta* is a true herbaceous plant, much coveted by flower arrangers. It will grow anything from 3 to 7 ft. tall, depending on soil and strain, and needs either very good support or none at all, in which latter case the whole plant will collapse under its own weight. This can look rather pretty, but is liable to cause some neighbouring group of plants to be smothered. The foliage of *C. recta* is capable of clinging to its supports, so that strong pea sticks are particularly efficient. The billowing white panicles of rather sickly-scented, cruciform flowers appear in June. They last only two or three weeks, but are followed by a decorative crop of seeds, and in any case the dark green foliage is always presentable. The variety *purpurea* has deep purple young foliage, which really does look tremendously handsome in spring. Later the purple colouring disappears and the flowers are pure white.

Another herbaceous species, already mentioned as a grandparent of Jackmanii, is *C. integrifolia*. When staked (it has no clinging device), it grows up to 3 ft. tall, but I prefer to grow it near low silver-leaved shrubs at the border front, e.g., *Helichrysum splendidum* or *Senecio cineraria*, and let it pick its way over and through them. When the plant is about 15 in. tall and looks as though it may get blown over sideways at any moment, you can give it a helping hand (or foot) by pushing some shoots one way, some another, in the required directions. It carries a succession of small indigo-blue lanterns over a long period from July to September. The variety *hendersonii* is larger flowered and taller growing (4 ft. plus), and should therefore be allowed to flop (if flopped it is allowed to be) over slightly taller shrubs such as *Phlomis fruticosa* or *Senecio laxifolius*. And so we come to *C.* × *eriostemon* (see Chapter 3, p. 21), with an abundance of small indigo lanterns. It

17. Proteus. Rosy-lilac.

18. Miss Crawshay. Pale rosy-mauve.

can grow up to 8 ft. tall, but should be tied to a post, as it is non-clinging, while the 6-ft. Durandii (Chapter 5, p. 37) can be treated either the same way or allowed to ramble at will—it is no smotherer and will not hurt neighbouring plants.

Another herbaceous or sub-shrubby group comprises three varieties of *C. heracleifolia*, viz., Campanile, Côte d'Azur and *davidiana*. They all have large, coarse trifoliate leaves, and axillary clusters of hyacinth-like pale bluish flowers from July to September. Campanile is a sub-shrub: that is, it makes herbaceous growth up to about 4 ft. which dies back at the end of the season to a woody stump. Actually, if you cut the plant down to the ground it does no harm. The pale bluish-mauve flowers are so prolific that they make one forget the foliage on a well-established plant. Côte d'Azur is very similar but the colouring is a little gluer and more intense; *davidiana* is truly herbaceous. It will gradually make a clump, and can be split up after a few years. It brows to about $3\frac{1}{2}$ ft. and can either have its shoots tied very loosely to one central stake or else be allowed its pleasure—all according to how formal is its setting. The latter method works well, for instance, when the clematis is planted among low shrub roses. The flowers of *davidiana* are pale but rather larger than those of the other two varieties, and from time to time flowering side shoots come off the main stems and are delightful to pick for the house, for this clematis, alone in its group, is heavily scented —not of hyacinths but just as strong.

A cross between *C. h.* var. *davidiana* and *C. recta*, made in Australia by Mr Russell V. Prichard, gave rise to Edward Prichard, introduced in 1950. It grows about 5 ft. tall and must be loosely tied to a stake, or looks well against a pillar. In the border it is liable, unless you are on the look-out for this trouble, to get swamped by its neighbours, for growth starts at ground level late in spring. Its terminal panicles of pale mauve, cruciform flowers, in August and September, are a great delight, and so is its scent.

An early cross between *C. flammula* and *C. integrifolia*, made in 1845, gave rise to *C.* × *aromatica* (syn. *C. coeruleo-odorata*). I had feared, when starting this book, that this variety had dropped out of cultivation, but am delighted to find that it has not, and is now in safe hands. Markham wrote of it as being suited to the hardy flower border and, indeed, it should be just the thing, making 6 ft. tall, non-clinging herbaceous shoots, and covering itself with deep violet flowers, about 1½ in. across, and with a markedly contrasting brush of white stamens. It is strongly scented.

FOR GROUND COVER AND TO
MASK TREE STUMPS

One's main aim, in choosing a clematis as ground cover, is that it shall do its job thoroughly. If it only half covers the ground, then weeds will gain a footing and they will be the harder to get out for the clematis shoots being in the way. Our native *C. vitalba* is a leafy plant and excellent for the purpose. In 1900 this species was crossed with *C. heracleifolia* var. *davidiana* and gave rise to the sub-shrubby *C. × jouiniana*, which is a first-rate ground coverer. It will make up to 12 ft. of non-clinging shoots annually, and carries axillary clusters of small blue-grey, cruciform flowers from early September. The variety *praecox* is more useful for general purposes, as its season starts in July. Although non-clinging, *C. × jouiniana* is quite adept at hoisting itself through and over neighbouring shrubs that happen to cross its path. *C. serratifolia* is another good enveloper. It belongs to the group of yellow clematis and carries flowers, late summer and autumn, shaped much like those of *C. tangutica*, but of a pale greenish-yellow which shows up less well. *C. tangutica, C. orientalis, C. rehderiana* and *C. flammula* are all suitable ground coverers.

Where tree stumps are in question, the above-mentioned clematis are just as appropriate, but the stumps' slight extra height of say 2 to 4 ft. above the surrounding ground level will also allow any of the small-flowered *viticella* hybrids already discussed in this chapter to be used effectively.

FOR EARLY SPRING DISPLAY

So as to be able to draw a line somewhere, I shall consider, here, those clematis which start to flower before *C. montana*. As with all spring flowers, their season may vary by as much as a month, from year to year, but they usually get into their swing just after the main daffodil season has finished, and before the end of April.

There are several good selections of *C. alpina* to choose from. They all breathe a wonderful freshness, with their flowers on tip-toe for flight, spangled against newly expanded foliage of palest green. Columbine is an effective light blue with an inner tube of small white staminodes. Pamela Jackman, a welcome newcomer, is a fine deep blue. Either of these would contrast splendidly with a vivid red 'Japonica' (*Chaenomeles*), or rambling among sprays of *Berberis stenophylla* or, again, as a backcloth to the yellow-green *Euphorbia palustris*. Ruby is a disappointing variant of *C. alpina*, since it tends to hide its blooms among the young foliage and, anyway, the colour is a rather drab amethyst. *C. alpina sibirica* is white but an improvement on this is White Moth, in which the staminodes are much enlarged, producing a small but fully double flower of great charm.

Clematis macropetala is a plumper version of *C. alpina*, and its staminodes are narrower than, but as long as, the sepals. *C. macropetala* itself opens with markedly lavender shading on the sepals but becomes bluer as it fades. In a good strain it is not inferior to Maidwell Hall, which is supposedly bluer. The lavender colouring is concentrated in a central area on the outside of the sepals; their margins, inner surface and all the visible staminodes being 'blue'. The mixture of these two shades is pleasant. Markham's Pink (syn. Markhamii) is not pink but a nice bright rosy-lilac.

Introduced by E. H. Wilson in 1900, *C. armandii* received the Royal Horticultural Society's Award of Garden Merit in 1938, so it enters these pages already loaded with honours. This species is evergreen, and since gardeners in general are crazy about evergreens, it starts off on the right foot. However, if we stopped to consider what the foliage of some of our evergreens looks like between January and April, we might prefer them deciduous. *C. armandii* comes to look passing dowdy at winter's end. Its trifoliate leaves consist of large tough leaflets which clatter like palm fronds in the breeze. When young and copper-coloured they are extraordinarily beautiful. The shrub is hardy enough in areas as cold as Birmingham, providing you give it a sunny, not too exposed wall. When happy, its vigour is terrific, and it will make young shoots 6 to 8 ft. long in every direction, except round its legs, which nearly always need covering up. So it will clothe a large area of south wall up to two or even three storeys high. The leafy trails of one year become the flower garlands of the next April, for a cluster of white, deliciously scented blossoms (each flower usually 2 in. across) arises from the axil of each leaf. Grown in a cool greenhouse or conservatory, it will flower in

March and scent the place out. There are two named selections of *C. armandii* marketed. Snowdrift has larger, purer white flowers than the type and is well worth getting if you can, but any old *armandii* is liable to get sold under this more attractive title. Then there is Apple Blossom. "Ah! What heaven!" you think, dreaming of clouds of tender pink, wafts of swooning fragrance, the blue spring sky, the cockle-warming sunshine, the birds, the bees, the butt—— Alas! it is not so. *C. armandii* Apple Blossom opens an indeterminate, grubby sort of pinkish-white, fades to white, but sometimes takes on a pinkish tinge again just before sepal-fall. (N.B. We speak of sepal-fall, *not* petal-fall in clematis jargon.)

Clematis indivisa is another evergreen, April-flowering species, which needs an even warmer, cosier spot and is hence even better suited to greenhouse cultivation. Its evergreen foliage is much smaller and less overwhelming than that of *armandii*. The axillary clusters of flower buds become apparent so early in spring that they are very vulnerable to frost. Beside its flowers, *C. armandii* looks plebeian indeed. They are perfectly spaced in *C. indivisa* and each slightly cupped bloom consists of six to eight spathulate sepals, overlapping at the base; the purest white with a central cushion of yellow stamens. The plants in cultivation are male, and often they are of the variety *lobata*, with toothed leaflets.

FOR AUTUMN DISPLAY

As the majority of clematis flower in high summer, it is useful to know which may be depended upon to make their main display either extra early or extra late. The main danger to late flowerers lurks in the earwig, and this is discussed in the chapter devoted to all such mar-joys.

Apart from clematis which make it their normal habit to flower late, it is possible to encourage most of the large-flowered hybrids which naturally expend their greatest efforts in May and June, to do so in August and September instead. These are the clematis which flower first on side-shoots from old wood made the year before; later, and less freely, at the tops of young shoots made the same year. If, instead of leaving the old wood to flower, you cut it hard back in late winter, the second crop will be far more generous. Those of us who realise the sacrifice entailed will seldom have the nerve to act, but supposing we know that we shall have to be absent from our homes in early summer, then this emergency plan should certainly go forward. It will work on any large-flowered hybrid that shows an inclination to flower late as well as early.

The clematis which naturally flower late anyway, have been discussed already under separate headings, and need merely to be enumerated here. Of the large types, we have Mme Baron-Veillard and Lady Betty Balfour in particular, while Belle Nantaise and W. E. Gladstone will carry right on from July to October. Even without special pruning, the second crop of Marie Boisselot is usually so good as to deserve mention here. Of the small-flowered hybrids, all the *texensis* group should be included, though their season may start as early as July. Of the species, we can choose from *C. flammula*, *C. paniculata* (extra late), *C. rehderiana*, *C. tangutica*, *C. orientalis*, *C. serratifolia* and *C. × jouiniana*.

FOR NORTH WALLS

The number of shrubs which will flourish and flower against a north wall is limited; so there is a special demand for clematis which will oblige in this way. However, it should be understood that there are north walls and north walls. Those which are exposed to the full force of the north-east winds, which so often prevail in spring and early summer, are no place for the average clematis, as their young shoots will get battered black. The *montana* group will put up with even these conditions, though. On the other hand a north wall which is sheltered from northerly winds can provide sanctuary for a wide selection of clematis. Quite how wide we cannot yet say, as information on this subject is scant. It seems probable that any of the large-flowered hybrids which do not positively demand a lot of sunshine lest they run entirely to wood and leaf (and I have already drawn attention to most of these) will do their stuff on a north wall. I should be naturally inclined to avoid, too, those varieties like Mme Grangé, Mme Edouard André and Jackmanii superba, whose colouring is so dark that they need sunlight to bring them to life. Contrari-wise, white clematis (and I can especially recommend Marie Boisselot here) shine with increased splendour from a north aspect, while blue clematis look all the bluer for not being seen in direct sunlight, but merely under the northern half of a blue sky. Then again, clematis such as the Nelly Moser sorority, which bleach unpleasantly in sunlight, can save their complexions against a sunless wall. (See also page 71 in pruning chapter.)

Of the species, *C. alpina*, *C. macropetala* and all their varieties are proven successful north-wallers, while the pale blossoms of *C. × jouiniana* (not forgetting the earlier-flowering form, *praecox*) are seen to great advantage on a north wall. Although this clematis is non-clinging, it is adept at working its way up to 12 ft. at least, behind strands of wire.

The evergreen *C. calycina* (syn. *C. balearica*) is especially well placed on a sheltered north wall. It will clothe a considerable area, up to 20 ft. high, with dark green foliage which changes (like many another evergreen) to rich bronzed tones in cold weather. The inch-wide, open-bell-shaped flowers appear over a long period starting in January, if mild, and continuing till early May. But I did not include this species among clematis for early spring display, since 'display' is hardly the word for a flower which is pale green with brown spots and could easily be missed by anyone not expecting it. Even so, we can say, without sarcasm, that it has its own charm. Another evergreen for the same sort of position is the nearly related *C. cirrhosa*, with off-white flowers borne throughout the same early season.

FOR SCENT

Clematis are fortunate in their public not expecting them to be scented, as it would expect every blessed rose to be, and so the cry 'Clematis don't smell like they used to' is mercifully never heard. Clematis which have scent bring it to those of us still possessed of a sense with which to savour it, as a bonus quality. Not many of them have it and most have been mentioned already, but it may be useful to gather them together here.

Of large-flowered hybrids, Fair Rosamond is the strongest (and not very strong at that), with The Queen and Duchess of Edinburgh as runners up. 'Between primroses and violets' is the classical definition of their scent. *C. afoliata* is said to be daphne-scented (which daphne?). *C. armandii* smells very good—I cannot say what of—while the vanilla scent of *C. montana* is delicious and far reaching. *C. recta* is strong and sickly, but flatters the senses of those who normally fail to smell anything. *C. flammula* is just like Meadow Sweet (*Filipendula ulmaria*) and admittedly on the sickly side, but delightful when wafted from a distance. Its offspring, *C.* × *aromatica* (*C. coeruleo-odorata*) is not quite so strong, but neither is it sickly; in fact it is very pleasing. *C. heracleifolia* var. *davidiana* is pleasant at not too close quarters. I cannot place the quality of its scent, which seems to belong to the perfumery. Edward Prichard smells strong and sweet. *C. paniculata* is scented, but I have not experienced it.

TO BE VIEWED ABOVE EYE LEVEL

A lot of clematis naturally tend to hang their heads. If it is the inside of the flower that we would like to see rather than the outside, then it is as well to plant these clematis so that we can look up at them. Among the hybrids, *C. viticella* is the parent chiefly responsible for this pensive attitude. Thus, most of the hybrids which are obviously rather close to *C. viticella*, e.g., Little Nell, Minuet, Abundance, *viticella rubra* and Alba Luxurians, can be best appreciated at or above eye level. The same may be said of Jackmanii (again thanks to the influence of *C. viticella* and, possibly also of *C. integrifolia*) and of very similar hybrids like Perle d'Azur, Star of India and Victoria.

When the outside of the sepals is just as bright and interesting as the inside, then it will not matter at what level we see their flowers. Such are *C. macropetala*, *C. alpina*, *C. tangutica* and *C. orientalis*.

TO BE VIEWED BELOW EYE LEVEL

Under the general sway of the Far Eastern species *C. patens*, *C. florida* and *C. lanuginosa*, we have a large range of hybrids with wide-open blooms that face upwards towards the sky. Now if we grow these against walls, the very presence of this dark background ensures that the clematis will hold their blooms obliquely outwards at such an angle that we can see them very well. But if they succeed in growing to the top of or above the wall, we shall see practically nothing of their flowers, and the same holds for clematis of this kind which we grow over tall shrubs, or pergolas or high poles. Of course, even this may not matter if steeply sloping or terraced ground, or a much used outlook from an upper storey window, allow us to take a bird's-eye view.

Failing such rather special circumstances, however, it will be sensible to grow these upward-looking clematis over low supports so that we can look down into their faces—an intimate association which is most rewarding. I have already given my opinion that clematis can look effective grown among the dwarfer types of heathers, and for this position I would suggest varieties like Etoile Violette or Venosa Violacea, which are good-tempered enough not to resent the competition of heather roots, but not so frantically vigorous as to be likely, in their turn, to swamp their partners.

Lowish growing shrubs like *Potentilla fruticosa*, *Cytisus praecox*, *Phlomis fruticosa*, lavender, rosemary, *Cistus corbariensis*, *Senecio laxifolius* and a hundred others, will make admirable supports for many of the less vigorous but largest flowered clematis hybrids, such as Crimson King, Lady Londesborough, Lincoln Star, Miss Bateman, Prins Hendrik, Miss Crawshay and Marcel Moser, to name but a random handful.

One may sometimes prefer a shrub or herbaceous plant to complete its own flowering before allowing it to be adorned with a clematis. This can be very successfully organised when the shrub flowers before midsummer and the clematis after. The clematis should then be planted behind the shrub or herbaceous group, and tied loosely to a pole of a length suitable to match its own vigour. Then, at the crucial moment when the shrub has done its stuff, the clematis is cut away from its support (which is removed), and draped forwards where it is required to flower. Suitable varieties would be Lady Betty Balfour, Belle Nantaise, Mme Baron-Veillard, W. E. Gladstone, Duchess of Sutherland, Ascotiensis—all upward-looking types.

19. Hagley Hybrid (rosy-mauve) with a climbing rose.

20. W. E. Gladstone. Lavender.

7

Cultivation

Before entering into details on how to grow clematis, it will probably be salutary to remind ourselves that thousands have been planted without preparation or aftercare, and yet have managed to give a good account of themselves. Such was my own experience with my oldest specimen of *C. florida bicolor*, generally reckoned as one of the more difficult clematis to satisfy. I was a good deal younger then, and I just planted it. Conditions were to its liking, apparently, for it has never given me a moment's uneasiness. It has grown 8 ft. high and is regularly covered with bloom for two to three months from the end of June. Admittedly I give it generous top-dressings of manure nowadays, but only as an afterthought.

However, it comes cheaper not to leave everything to chance, and anyway it is more interesting to understand one's plants, their likes and their dislikes.

SOILS, WATERING AND FEEDING

To the all-demanding question 'What do clematis like?' the short answer is 'Everything you can give them'. And I find it helpful to add that if clematis are accorded the same cultural treatment as most gardeners would give their hybrid tea roses, they will be well satisfied.

Clematis are most easily grown on rather heavy, water-retentive soils. Clay soils suit them very well so long as the pure clay itself is not too near the surface and as long as drainage is adequate. The most difficult clematis soils are those like the Bagshot or Folkestone sands which are 'hungry', i.e., deficient in soil nutrients, and which dry out terribly quickly. Equally difficult are thin chalk soils, with solid chalk not far below the surface, as one finds it on the slopes of the Downs. Here again, the main trouble is from water shortage.

Even that greatest of gardeners, Gertrude Jekyll, found the large-flowered clematis hybrids difficult to grow on her light, sandy soil at Godalming. I should like to quote the entire paragraph from *Colour in the Flower Garden* (published by Country Life Ltd. in 1908) in which she tells us this. It is not all directly relevant to the subject under discussion, but it is instinct with such gardening wisdom as we may never meet again:

'Delphiniums, which are indispensable for July, leave bare stems with quickly yellowing leafage when the flowers are over. We plant behind them the white Everlasting Pea, and again behind that Clematis Jackmanii. When the Delphiniums are over, the rapidly forming seed-pods are removed, the stems are cut down to just the right height, and the white Peas are trained over them. When the Peas go out of bloom in the middle of August, the Clematis is brought over. It takes some years for these two plants to become established; in the case of those I am describing the Pea has been four or five years planted and the Clematis seven. They cannot be hurried, indeed in my garden it is difficult to get the Clematis to grow at all. But good gardening means patience and dogged determination. There must be many failures and losses, but by always pushing on there will also be the reward of success. Those who do not know are apt to think that hardy flower gardening of the best kind is easy. It is not easy at all. It has taken me half a life-time merely to find out what is best worth doing, and a good slice out of another half to puzzle out the ways of doing it.'

There is little of Miss Jekyll's book which is not as well worth reading today as at the time she wrote it. Nevertheless, gardeners have continued to accumulate knowledge which was not available to her then and I believe that, if she were alive now, Miss Jekyll would have been growing clematis more successfully than was possible sixty years ago. Appreciation of the importance of watering during dry spells between April and September has caused the most radical change to gardening technique in the past half century and water is undoubtedly the limiting factor where success with clematis is in question. As a rough-and-ready guide to the quantity required, I would suggest an inch of water every ten days for a plant growing in an open situation; twice this amount for a clematis growing against a wall. You need only to know how much rain has fallen during each ten-day period to work out the deficit that is to be made good. Many gardeners think they have watered a plant when, in fact, they have merely tickled its foliage. It should revolutionise their standards to remind them that one inch of water requires $4\frac{1}{2}$ gallons per square yard. The more finely it is put on, the better, and it is obviously useless to slosh it on so heavily that the soil pans and cannot absorb it.

As watering also has the effect of washing nutrients away, each application should automatically be followed up with a dose of fertiliser—either soot water or manure water or, more simply, the same general fertiliser as you may be using for, say, your tomatoes.

There is a widespread but quite unfounded belief (I had almost said superstition) among gardeners that clematis like chalk soils, and that under acid or neutral conditions lime should be added. This legend has been repeated in practically every book or article written on clematis in the last hundred years. When I tried to explode it in the gardening press, I was taken severely to task by one reader, whose offensive tactics were to quote all the leading clematis authorities of the past sixty years against me. If only people would trust the expert less and the evidence of their own eyes more! It is my experience that clematis will thrive in very acid soil conditions if they are well provided with their water and other nutrient requirements. Indeed, it seems to matter little to them what the acidity of their soil may be within wide limits. But for gardeners to get the idea that because, for example, they are working on a calcareous soil, *ergo* clematis will revel in it, is to start off on the wrong foot and is likely to lead to disappointment. The clematis probably will not care whether the soil is limy or not, but the fact that most calcareous soils are free draining and liable to drought will make it harder to grow clematis well, not simpler.

Of course, it is easy to see how the myth grew up. Our only native clematis, *C. vitalba*, is usually found growing wild on chalk or limestone soils. Jumping from the particular to the general, gardeners assumed that all clematis must therefore need calcareous soils. One would be reaching a similar, though more disastrous, conclusion by assuming that, because *Rhododendron hirsutum* is a native of limestone regions, therefore all rhododendrons need lime! And I might add that *C. vitalba* is not noticeably less happy when introduced to an acid garden soil. Indeed, I cannot think of a single tree or shrub which, in order to prosper under garden conditions in this country, will anywhere need the addition of lime to its soil.

PLANTING

Clematis are most readily obtained from nurseries in autumn and in spring up to, say, mid-June. But there is no close season for their planting other than the weather. If the ground is sodden or frozen, you will obviously defer operations, but there is no transplanting problem, as any young clematis worth buying will be pot grown, and turning it out of a pot need not involve damaging its roots.

The spirit in which to set about preparing the planting site is by trying to visualise your clematis full grown and in the full glory of its display, and repeating this miracle for you year after year for perhaps upwards of fifty years. It will not then be hard to imagine what a drain on the soil's resources will be involved. Yet once the clematis is there you are powerless to alter soil conditions except by top dressings; it will not even be safe to fork around its roots. for these will come almost to the surface.

Except where the soil is already in splendid condition to a depth of 2 ft., it is worth excavating a hole 18 in. or 2 ft. square, and 2 ft. deep. The top soil is laid on one side and the unpleasant sub-soil is barrowed away. If it is a clay or silt sub-soil there may be drainage troubles, for excavated holes, even when filled in again, are liable to act as sumps. Where necessary, then, 4-in. tile drains should be laid at a depth of about 18 in. and led along a gentle downward slope to a convenient soak-away. The tiles are laid on the bed of the trench and are then covered with a layer of shingle or other like coarse material so as to prevent the drain from silting up.

In filling up the hole, the top soil will go back and, into the bottom half, a good supply of well-rotted farmyard manure or black compost from the heap, which the clematis roots will find when they grow down to it. Peat, too, can be liberally mixed in throughout. I remember being amazed to see the reaction of a *C. macropetala* which had been planted behind a young camellia

4. Ville de Lyon

5. Marie Boisselot
(*syn.* Mme Le
Coultre)

6. Belle Nantaise

7. This specimen of
   Victoria has a
   pole as support

in a large pocket of almost pure peat. The clematis had gone mad with joy and thrown up suckers (true to type) in every direction and at a considerable distance from its main stem. Once-used John Innes potting compost is excellent material for hole filling and a couple of handfuls of bone meal or hoof-and-horn worked in will be a good slow-acting fertiliser. As the hole fills, so its contents should be packed firmly down with your heel, and before it is quite topped up, the centre of the hole can be marked with a stick where the clematis is to be planted.

Young clematis will nearly always be pot-bound, i.e., when turned out of the pot, practically nothing but roots will be visible and the plant will be panting for room to expand. This should be no cause for surprise or complaint. An interval of perhaps only six weeks will elapse between the time when its roots have not yet filled their pot (and if you try to plant the clematis at this stage, all the pot soil will fall away from the roots while in transit or while you handle them) and when they have so thoroughly filled it as to be ready for more room. A nurseryman cannot be expected to sell each clematis during the brief interval between these extremes. It may have to await its turn for months afterwards.

As long as the clematis has an abundance of healthy roots on its arrival, there is nothing to worry about. They are thick and round, rather like leather bootlaces, where the large-flowered hybrids are concerned, and you should, before planting, gently unwind and pull them downwards from their state of spiral congestion.

If the ball of roots seems the slightest bit dry, it should be stood in a bucket of water for five or ten minutes. Not only will this make the roots easier to unravel, but it is difficult—almost impossible, in fact—to moisten a ball of dry roots once they have been planted.

The main danger to watch against while the clematis is actually being planted, is that the cane to which its stem is tied does not become separated at its base from the root system, and thereby take on a semi-detached life of its own. When this happens, the clematis can get severely kinked at the base of its stem. Actually, this damage is often more apparent than real, and it is surprising how violently you can kink a clematis stem without cutting off supplies to the main shoot or setting it back in any way.

I recommend planting about an inch deeper than the clematis

E

was growing in its pot. This encourages it to make roots from the lowest nodes so buried, and if 'wilt' attacks the stem at soil level, new shoots are the more likely to be thrown up from underground.

When planted, the clematis needs to be firmed in with the whole weight of your body behind your fists and then (almost always) given a thorough watering to settle the new soil around the roots.

Except for the most robust species, all clematis must have shade at their roots. The most satisfactory way to provide them with this is from the shade cast by neighbouring shrubs or cushion-forming plants like catmint, helianthemums or *Anthemis cupaniana*. Paving stones will also keep them cool at the base. However, stone slabs laid flat sometimes encourage ants to nest beneath them, in which case it is better to make an inverted V with two tiles or slates where the sun would strike on the clematis roots.

When a clematis is being planted at the foot of a wall, it should be borne in mind that this is probably the driest spot in the whole garden. And a north wall is just about as dry as a south, because although the former does not meet the sun's baking influence, neither does it have the moist south-westerlies blowing rain against its face. Walls are nearly always built of porous materials and they lap up moisture from the ground near them with alarming thoroughness. So, wherever space allows, your clematis should be planted 15 in. forward from the wall and then trained back on to it.

I have already written (p. 30) of the dangers of greedy root systems from neighbouring plants competing with clematis for nutrients and moisture. I will merely and briefly repeat here that a clematis should be planted as far as possible from the source of such roots and, when they belong to the shrub or tree over which the clematis is to climb, the latter must be led from a distance on to its host's branches, by way of connecting strings. When planted in turf, the clematis must be guarded against the rapaciousness of grass by keeping a circle of 2 ft. radius weed- and turf-free round its base, heavily mulching and watering this area the while.

ROUTINE MAINTENANCE

The only necessary (and, indeed, the only possible) cultural attention which you need give to clematis is by continually preventing unnecessary competition from neighbouring plants;

by giving them water and liquid feeds whenever they need them and by applying in winter an annual surface mulch to the soil above their roots. Clematis roots will be found in the soil surface at a distance of 8 to 10 ft. from the trunk of a well-established specimen of even a not-so-vigorous hybrid type. Grown in a border with other hungry plants, it is easy to manure them all at the same time; less easy, perhaps, for the over-keen gardener to remember not to get busy with his fork. When the top-dressing is of some rich substance like manure from a deep-litter chicken house, or farmyard manure which has not been exposed to the weather and thus had half its goodness washed out of it, then it will do a good job without the further addition of bone meal or hoof-and-horn in the spring. The latter should be added where a boost is needed, though I confess to using this material as a top-dressing most reluctantly, since it all seems to go to supplementing the diet of our local house sparrow population and also of my insatiable dachshunds.

8

Pruning and Training

An unpruned clematis looks like a disembowelled mattress—a sorry sight. From year to year its owner grows more despairing; his only comfort is that the birds are nesting in the tangle and perhaps not all of them are sparrows. Every time he bumps into this dropsical mass, his face, his neck, his clothes get sprayed with water-drops. He loves clematis but he abhors this loathsome abortion. What is he to do?

The trouble with clematis is that they cannot all be pruned the same way. For the busy man who has not the time to go into why's and wherefores, my kindest policy, at this stage, is to lay down three basic pruning methods, one of which will apply to almost any clematis he may grow.

Method A. Immediately after flowering cut out all shoots that have flowered. This applies to the small-flowered species and their varieties which bloom in April and May, e.g., *C. montana, C. macropetala, C. alpina* and *C. armandii*.

Method B. Cut out dead growth. Separate and train the remaining shoots, shortening them back to the first pair of strong buds. Time of pruning: February–March. This applies to all those large-flowered hybrids which start flowering *before* mid-June, e.g., Ville de Lyon, Nelly Moser, Lasurstern, Beauty of Worcester, Belle of Woking and Marie Boisselot.

Method C. Cut all shoots hard back in February to early March, to a strong pair of buds, 3 ft. or less above ground level. This applies to those species and hybrids which start flowering *after* mid-June, e.g., *C. flammula, C. tangutica,* Comtesse de Bouchaud, Jackmanii and Mme Edouard André.

68

21. Mme Baron-Veillard (rosy-lilac) on a north wall, late September.

22. Durandii. Rich indigo blue.

In the alphabetical descriptive list at the end of this book, an A, B or C will be found attached to each species or hybrid to which one of these pruning methods can be applied. This is all that needs to be known by anyone wishing to work to a quick rule of thumb.

However, there must be many readers who, like myself, object to doing a thing without knowing the reason why, and in any case there are plenty of variations on these basic pruning methods, so I shall consider each of them again in greater detail.

While there is no harm in practising Method A every year, there is often no need. If, for instance, you want *C. montana* or *C. macropetala* to cover a large area of garage roof, it will be sufficient to give a severe pruning once in four or five years. But in this case, not only the trails of growth that have just flowered will have to be removed, but a lot of dead wood also. If these ultra-vigorous species are required to cover no more than a small area, however, their pruning should be annual, otherwise it will become impossible to keep them within bounds.

These clematis flower on shoots made in the previous year. It is because they are so very early flowering that they can be hard pruned immediately afterwards (at the end of May, say) and still have the whole summer and autumn before them in which to grow abundant new shoots for next year's display of blossom.

Many gardeners do not think of trimming their montanas until after the first hard winter's frost—usually in December—has suddenly stripped them of their leaves. If they realised that every healthy shoot removed in winter was thirty or fifty of next spring's flowers destroyed, they might desist.

The clematis to which we apply Method B flower later and are, by and large, of weaker growth. But, like those in the first group, they produce their flowers on wood made in the previous year (or, to be more exact, on short side-shoots off this wood), and plenty of this must be retained when pruning. The separating of shoots is admittedly tedious; you must set about the job in a spirit of patience (and in not too paralysingly cold weather), snip-snipping at every old tendril that linked this tangled skein. But the results justify the labour, for the clematis can then be organised to cover the largest possible area and every bloom will be carried separate from its neighbours so that it can be enjoyed to the full. A skein of shoots that has not been disentangled results in many blooms being partially or wholly hidden in the welter of their own making.

Most clematis hybrids start very early into growth and in mild winters may carry young shoots several inches long by the end of February. Late winter is chosen as the time for pruning the group under discussion because signs of life are sufficiently apparent by then for distinguishing the dead shoots, which must be extracted, from the living. Furthermore, each shoot will have its weak tip removed, taking it back to a pair of strong buds. Not till late winter can one see which buds are strong. Now, the strongest *looking* and most forward pair of buds at this season are, in fact, weak. It is the next pair of buds below them, still almost dormant, that are really strong. Just above these the cut is made.

Clematis pruned by Method C are expected to carry all their blossom on young shoots made in the current season. At pruning, then, all the previous season's old shoots can be entirely cut away. We say that they should be taken back to a pair of strong buds. In fact, any pair of buds which we cut back to at this low level will be made strong by the very act of cutting back to them, although at the time of doing so they will be small, insignificant and utterly dormant.

The time for this pruning is again appointed for late winter. That is the text-book instruction, but it fails to take any account of our feelings, by expecting us to endure for four months the billowing mess of old shoots which is especially obtrusive in clematis of this group. On a well-established plant you can, in fact, make a practice of pruning it in late autumn. The danger, you may be told, is that its important shoots will be lured into premature growth in a mild mid-winter spell, only to be frosted later. Well, I can vouch that, even if this happens, other buds will be forthcoming to take the place of those which were snatched untimely. Anyone who really dislikes the risks of early pruning can compromise by taking two bites at the cherry: cut only the most unsightly tangle away in autumn and finish the job off in late winter.

When one of these Method C clematis is being grown up a pole, the lower you prune the better, as more height will thereby be allowed for the young shoots' development. But supposing the clematis is required to climb up the 20-ft. wall of a building or into a tree of similar height: if you then prune it down to, say,

1 ft. annually, it cannot be expected to make the grade. The procedure here should be to prune hard when the plant is young, but each year thereafter to cut it back a little less, until there is finally a framework of woody old shoots up to a height of the first 6 ft. or so. It may become necessary to disguise these bare lower portions with some other shrub or different type of clematis.

A further refinement in pruning by Method C arises when the clematis is required to cover a considerable *length* of wall. If we cut everything back to 6 in., it will be quite impossible to separate and train the young growths as they develop, without damaging them. They will all run up together, arm in arm, and flower in a bundle at the top, occupying precious little wall space in the process. The way to prune in this case is to cut the shoots back by different amounts: some hard, some so as to leave as much as 6 ft. of old growth, and others to intermediate lengths. Then they can be trained out to right and to left, near ground level and almost horizontally. The young shoots will, as always, develop from the extreme pair of buds above which each cut was made and will run up the wall like the prongs of a fork, covering a large area.

FIG. 2. COVERING A WALL. Each shoot is cut back to a different length (shown by heavy lines); they will then grow upwards from the buds at the tips.

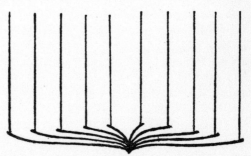

Clematis pruned by Method C tend to be less suitable for north walls than those pruned by Methods A and B. North walls being dark, Group C clematis will always tend to rush up as high as they can in search of light at the top of the wall, and flower out of sight, leaving a lot of ugly stems where we should like to see flowers. The advantage of clematis flowering on old wood in Groups A and B is that, wherever they may have made their growth during the summer, we can train it against the wall where we want it, during the dormant season, and be sure that it will flower in this position, come spring and early summer.

YOUNG STOCK

The routine recommendations for newly planted stock is to prune back to a pair of buds 6 in. to 1 ft. above ground level, at the end of winter. For autumn-planted clematis this is, indeed, a sound general precept. The balance between root and shoot growth should, in these early stages, favour the roots. I would make an exception of *montana*-type clematis, however, since they are vigorous enough to be allowed to flower in their first spring.

When clematis are spring-planted, they will already have received their first pruning in the nursery and the customer will not need to do anything more about this. By the time the following winter/spring arrives, the clematis will be established and can be treated in the usual way according to its category.

23. *C. montana rubens* (rosy-mauve) covering a wall.

24. *C. montana rubens* growing over a wire framework.

25. *C. chrysocoma*. Soft pinkish-mauve.

26. *C. rehderiana.* Straw yellow.

27. *C. flammula*. Pure white.

9

Clematis Troubles

It is customary to open a chapter on this subject with a reassuring declaration (while touching wood all round) that clematis are mercifully exempt from all but the merest handful of pests and diseases. Well, maybe this is so compared to the string of ailments which roses, potatoes and sheep are heirs to. All the same, I would say that the gardener who succeeds in establishing three out of every four large-flowered hybrid clematis planted has reason to be pleased with himself. The nurseryman's losses are even higher, for a young clematis is at its most vulnerable.

'WILT'

The word 'wilt', in inverted commas, is liberally sprinkled through these pages, and it is the Clematis Wilt Disease which brings 90 per cent of the grey hairs to every clematis grower's head, be he amateur or professional. If there were money in clematis; if they were big business in the way that roses, potatoes and sheep are, then we may be sure that the necessary research would have been carried out to discover what causes the disease (we do not know this, even) and hence, how to control it.[1] As matters rest, however, we are almost as ignorant on the subject today as we were a hundred years ago when the trouble first made its appearance and eventually caused such anxiety and disappointment as to put a heavy damper on the initial enthusiasm which had greeted the introduction of the large-flowered hybrids. For it is this type of clematis which is affected. The species and small-flowered hybrids are so vigorous as to be virtually immune.

This fatal ignorance among us all has led to an almost super-

[1] Since writing these words, it has at last been decided to investigate the causes of 'wilt' at one of the research stations.

73

stitious dread of the disease. Many nurserymen, I have noticed, will not even dare to mention it to a customer. How tired they must be of the ominous opening words: 'I bought a clematis from you last year.' 'Yes, madam?' defensively, apprehensively, and then the inevitable sequel: 'It died.' The timing of its death will vary in different cases, but the dismaying suddenness of collapse is invariable. The customer is outraged, insulted, mystified. 'It was growing so well,' she (or he) protests, 'and I did everything you say in your instructions; shaded and mulched its roots, kept it well watered. Where did I go wrong?'

At a Chelsea Flower Show I listened, fascinated, to one of these familiar exchanges (in which I am so often personally involved) at the stand of a specialist clematis firm. Everything the good lady described spoke unequivocally of clematis 'wilt', yet the firm's representative never breathed a suggestion of this as being the cause of the trouble. It was unfair of him, I thought, and yet he probably knew that to offer an explanation without a remedy would give no satisfaction.

The symptoms of 'wilt', then, are frequently only too obvious. From being at one moment in, apparently, perfect health, the whole of a young plant down to ground level suddenly collapses and dies. If the plant has more than one shoot, only one may be affected. People sometimes think that it has died from the top downwards but this is not so. Only because the top of the shoot is softest, do the symptoms become apparent here first. The trouble, in fact, has occurred just at ground level where a fungus (?) has attacked the stem and rotted it through.

'Wilt' often occurs during the kind of warm, encouraging spell in May when one can almost hear things growing, they are moving so fast. But it can also happen at any other stage of the growing season. Neither are winter losses inconsiderable, though they may or may not be due to the same cause. Only young plants with thin stems are endangered. Having built up a woody stem after three or four years, a plant can be considered safe.

We do not know what fungus, or other pathogen, causes the disease. In America, a somewhat similar but not identical affliction has been ascribed to the fungus (named after its host) *Aschochyta clematidina*. But this has not yet been isolated from 'wilted' clematis in Britain. My own unsubstantiated suspicions fall on our old enemy the Grey Mould fungus, *Botrytis cinerea*. It is so

like it to enter living plant tissue by way of a damaged or dead
leaf stalk, of which there are always some at the base of a clematis
stem, since the large-flowered types never shed their leaves cleanly.
Against this is the evidence that the fungus sometimes does its
damage not at the node but between nodes. Incidentally, *C.
armandii*, although small flowered, vigorous and woody, often
has its branches of the current season attacked by a fungus which
causes conspicuous dark brown patches in the greenish stems,
eventually encircling them and killing their distal portions.
Whether or not this is another aspect of the same disease, I wish
I knew.

'Wilt' is of widespread occurrence. It is as likely to occur on
virgin soil where clematis have never been grown before, as
elsewhere. Neither does the nurseryman's cultivation of young
stock in sterilised soil minimise the onslaught. An awful lot of
rubbish has been written about grafted clematis plants being more
liable to wilt than those raised from cuttings. I have raised
umpteen thousands of clematis from cuttings and I am quite
certain that my losses among them from 'wilt' are no fewer than
those experienced by nurseries which mainly practice grafting.
Indeed, I know one nursery which grafts most of its clematis and
apparently never experiences 'wilt'. They are as mystified by their
good fortune as I am. Their stock usually spends its whole life, till
sold, under glass, but this is no protection against the disease, as
other nurserymen will vouch.

If we spray the base of our young clematis with a fungicide at
frequent intervals through the growing season, it may do some
good. There is no evidence or proof that it will, but as an act of
faith it is certainly worth performing if it makes the performer
feel better. Another rite which is commonly observed is the
immediate removal of the wilted stem. Give it a sharp tug and it
will usually break asunder at the base where the rot occurred. Its
removal does at least look better than leaving the corpse on the
scene. But leaving it does not seem to inhibit the plant from
throwing a new shoot at the base, if that was its intention.

This, then, is chief among the crumbs of comfort which I can
scatter. A 'wilted' plant can and often does (perhaps half the time)
recover. Especially if it was planted rather deeply, as recommended in the last chapter, it may gladden us by sending up a new
shoot. You must not give up hope of this happening too quickly,

for there may be an interval of three or four months between death and resurrection. In the meantime keep the plant well watered and your fingers crossed. Often a plant will 'wilt' a second time, and then a third. This suggests that it is unhappy. Sun on its roots, incidentally, strongly predisposes clematis to 'wilt'. It is wise to take the hint which the plant is screaming at you and try it somewhere else. I have known this to work like a charm. Indeed, charms are one's strongest hope when ignorance precludes the use of scientific method.

MILDEW

Next to 'wilt', all other clematis troubles pale into insignificance. In the kind of summer (usually dry and sometimes hot) when your roses and Michaelmas daisies are being afflicted with powdery mildew, some of your clematis may be similarly attacked, and by the same fungi. The trouble usually becomes apparent in July and is therefore most serious on certain clematis whose flowering season is just getting into its stride then, e.g., Jackmanii, Mme Edouard André, Durandii, Star of India and the *texensis* hybrids. Leaves, stems and flowers are all affected, first with scattered silvery-grey spots, and later with a uniformly grey coating. The parasite can have a most debilitating effect on its host, reducing both its growth and the size of its flowers, while the latter's true colouring is quite masked. Fortunately the attack of one year is not carried forward into the next. I do not mean by this that mildew is not still present, ready to pounce. It is, but so entirely at the weather's command, that unless the season favours mildew for two years running, a clematis which is in wretched condition one summer can be healthy and radiant the next.

Clematis known to be susceptible (and this excludes such late-flowering species as *C. flammula*, *C. rehderiana*, *C. tangutica* and *C. orientalis*) should be grown for preference in open, sunny situations where the air circulates freely about them; not in the stagnant kind of atmosphere prevailing against walls. Control can also be gained by spraying with the same fungicide as is recommended against mildew on roses—Karathane is the chemical of the moment, but there will doubtless be improvements. It should be applied at the end of June and again a month later.

28. *C. texensis*. This red-flowered species is one of the parents of such varieties
as Countess of Onslow and Gravetye Beauty.

29. *C. tangutica* (seed heads and blooms). Butter yellow.

VIRUSES

Virus disease in clematis has not been investigated. Its presence can only be presumed and, from the evidence of one's eyes, is highly probable. I have, for instance, an old plant of Mrs Cholmondeley whose young foliage is invariably mottled with a pale and darker green mosaic, while the outline of the leaves is frequently distorted. As the leaves mature, so the symptoms become masked and the plant is not prevented from growing well and flowering freely.

A condition often encountered in the double, white Duchess of Edinburgh leads to many of its outer sepals being much enlarged and green, so that it becomes impossible to say where the last leaves end and the first sepals begin. The whole flower is grossly disfigured. This again would appear to be a virus effect.

It often happens that, whereas a plant may remain in relatively good health when infected by one virus only, it can break down when attacked by a complex of several viruses simultaneously. This could well be the reason for some of the older clematis cultivars having fallen out of favour due to a general weakening of their constitution which makes them particularly difficult to propagate and to manage in the early stages of cultivation. The weakening effect of viruses on young stock could also predispose them to 'wilt'.

If we are to learn at some future date, as has happened with so many other vegetatively propagated plants, that nearly all nursery stock is virus infected, we should not allow this to cause us sleepless nights. For it will then be true to say that a great many of the robuster clematis hybrids are able to grow and flower well despite their handicap, and this is all that really matters.

EARWIGS

Apart from the grotesque kind of hazards occasioned by rabbits, hares, deer, dogs and clumsy gardeners, against which it is not my business to suggest remedies here, the most serious clematis pest is the earwig. Populations of this insect build up throughout the summer, and from July till autumn they constitute an annual menace to clematis in the majority of gardens. They will eat young foliage till nothing remains of a shoot except a skeleton of stalks and midribs, and, if the plant succeeds in producing flowers, earwigs will quickly eat great holes and gashes out of their sepals. Unless something is done to control them, the later-flowering clematis are scarcely worth growing.

Gardeners are mainly of diurnal habits; if they go into their gardens at night, it is to saunter and to sniff at their tobacco plants, not to search for pests. They often fail, in consequence, to identify the cause of the trouble which reveals itself only too plainly on their clematis by day. Indeed, it is surprising to find that textbooks devoted to the clematis often omit any reference to earwigs. Yet you have only to pull aside a folded or overlapping sepal to find them snugly roosting, in daytime, while torchlight will reveal them dangling in hordes as they revel in their midnight feasts.

Control is most simply achieved by spraying stems and leaves at three-weekly intervals with a DDT or BHC preparation, or a mixture of both. These leave a persistent deposit which will poison the earwigs when they walk over it.

SLUGS

Slugs and snails are most troublesome to young plants. They eat away their tender shoots at or below ground level. They will even skin and eventually destroy not-so-young shoots, about a year old, which have begun to get woody but are not yet woody enough. The most insidious type of slug is the small, black one which spends its life underground, persistently chomping and chewing throughout the winter months while the clematis are resting and our own thoughts are rather consciously avoiding the garden at its most unpleasant season. Particularly after a wet summer and autumn, and on heavy soils, when there has been an impressive build-up of slugs, clematis which were autumn-planted tend to disappear.

In these circumstances, it is best to plant in spring. If the clematis arrive in autumn, having been ordered before you realised how wet and slug-favouring it was going to be, you can pot them up and keep them in a cold greenhouse or plunge them in ashes outside for the winter.

It is difficult to reach subterranean slugs with baits, but they are otherwise dealt with in the normal ways, using a metaldehyde preparation.

10

Propagation

I find it amusing to reflect that in the first book on clematis, written by Moore and Jackman in the 1870s, the subject of propagation was not even mentioned. Such was the professional secrecy jealously maintained by nurserymen about their methods. Nowadays they mostly appreciate that these taboos are unnecessary. Thus Mr Fisk, in 1962, tells his readers, with the detail of a professional's personal experience, just how to propagate their clematis, whether it be by cuttings, layers, grafting or from seed. Most gardeners today are amateurs. To gain their interest and participation in every aspect of gardening profits the nurseryman far more in the long run than he stands to lose because they have learnt to 'do it themselves'. Besides, this more liberal view of the matter engenders a spirit of confidence between professional and amateur which is of the greatest value.

The most interesting development in clematis propagation during the past fifteen years has been the swing-over from grafting to cuttings as a commercial method. Formerly, almost every clematis marketed had been grafted. A few, like *C. montana*, which root especially easily from cuttings, or like *C. armandii*, which are especially difficult to graft, were the only exceptions. At the present, at least three specialist clematis nurseries do all their propagating by cuttings; others still do a higher proportion by grafting. Whether all commercial propagation will eventually be by cuttings, I am unable to prophesy. Grafting has its own advantages. I think it possible that one may be able to obtain a strong plant of some of the weaker varieties, like Duchess of Edinburgh or *C. florida bicolor*, more easily by grafting than from cuttings. I say this tentatively, as I do all my own propagating by cuttings and have not made comparative experiments.

GRAFTING

For years the notion has been put about by private gardeners like
William Robinson, Ernest Markham (in particular) and their
successors to the present day, that grafted plants are so much
harder to establish than *plants on their own roots* and that it is a
wicked practice on the nurseryman's part to continue with the
former method. The complaint, however, is based on a mis-
conception so simple that we are left to marvel at their ignorance.

A clematis is not, like a rose, grafted on to a rootstock which
will become the plant's root system for its whole life. A clematis is
nurse-grafted: that is to say, a bud of the desired variety (the
scion) is grafted on to a piece of root of any other convenient
variety (the stock), just to give the former a start. Shortly after
union, the scion will make its own roots; those of the stock will
gently fade away. The latter scarcely ever takes charge. On the
contrary, it should live only long enough to get the scion started.
By the time a grafted plant reaches the customer, the desired
variety *is already on its own roots* and you have a product in no
way differing from one that was raised from a cutting.

There are occasional cases where the roots of the stock are
peculiarly strong, and the scion is never properly able to establish
its own root system. This is the only time when grafting may
justifiably be termed a bad practice—because badly practised.

The most commonly used stocks for grafting are *C. viticella* and
C. vitalba. However, it is perfectly possible to use pieces of root
of any of the large-flowered hybrids. Being thick, they are quite
easy to handle but will not give rise to a strong plant as quickly
as will one of the ultra-vigorous species. In this country, seedlings
of *C. vitalba* are most widely in use. Seed is drilled in rows outside
and the seedlings are generally ready for grafting in their second
year. They are lifted in batches from January onwards and can be
packed in sphagnum moss and given bottom heat to get them
active. Meantime, the stock plants for producing scion wood are
brought on in a warm glasshouse and the trails of young shoots
are ready when about a yard long and with, say, five nodes firm
enough to graft with. Five nodes will yield ten scions if each is
split longitudinally into two. Or you may prefer to give yourself
a double chance on each graft by making only one scion from each
node, thus retaining both buds.

30. *C. orientalis* L. & S. 13342. Bright yellow.

31. *C. recta*. White.

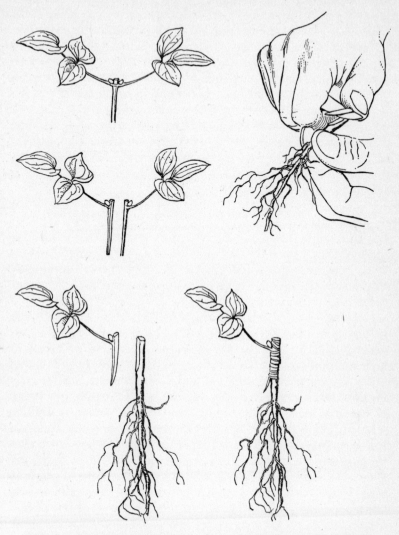

FIG. 3. GRAFTING CLEMATIS. *Clematis viticella* and *C. vitalba* are
the most commonly used stocks for grafting, but pieces of root of any
large-flowered hybrid can be used. The selected scion wood is split
down the middle and the bud on each portion can be used for grafting.
The scion is secured to the stock with thin, wet raffia and the grafted
plant potted with the scion bud below soil level. The pot is then placed
in a closed case with bottom heat.

F

A simple whip graft is the most common, making the cuts about an inch long or less. On a seedling stock the cut is made on the hypocotyl—that is the (usually straight) piece of stem just above the roots and below the first pair of leaves (actually the cotyledons). There can be no question of suckers arising from this part of the stock. The graft is tied with thin, wet raffia but not waxed, and the grafted plants potted with the scion bud below soil level and put in a closed case with bottom heat. Overwatering at this stage will result in heavy losses from damping off. After the union has been made in about three or four weeks' time, the plants are hardened off and staked as necessary. They will be of saleable size, if grafted in early spring, by late summer, but there's many a slip . . .

CUTTINGS

Propagation by cuttings will have a much wider appeal among amateurs than by grafting, yet is by no means straightforward where the large-flowered hybrids are concerned. The method would have gained currency eighty years earlier in commercial circles, had it been simple.

But first I should, perhaps, explain about nodal and internodal cuttings and when to use which. A nodal cutting consists of two nodes (or joints). The cuts are made immediately below the lower node and immediately above the upper. The lower node is buried in the rooting medium and the upper node should, ideally, be at the soil surface. However, the distance between nodes in a length of clematis stem is often great. Six to nine inches is nothing unusual. This stretch of bare stem between nodes is the internode. It is fortunate that a clematis is as ready to make roots from a cut made at any point along the internode as it is from a nodal cut. Hence the internodal cutting, which is much the most common kind. In this case, then, a cut is again made above a node but the lower cut is made at a convenient distance below the same node— usually about an inch or 1½ in. below, when the wood is soft, but 4 or 5 in. below in a hardwood cutting. The cutting is then inserted in its rooting medium, generally in a pot, and it is easy to arrange for the node to rest at soil level, as it should. An internodal cutting has the further advantage of being twice as economical in material as the nodal type, since only one node is used instead of two.

There are two ways in which I have successfully rooted hard-wood internodal cuttings, about 4 in. long, and one way in which I have failed to root them. The first success, using Perle d'Azur and Nelly Moser, was by inserting the cuttings in December round the rim of $4\frac{1}{2}$-in. long-tom pots, and keeping them in a cold frame. The frame was fully ventilated throughout, but the cuttings were always in a shaded spot. The cutting compost consisted of one part by bulk of sterilised loam, two parts of peat and three parts grit (sand). The rooted cuttings were ready to pot up by the following autumn, so the process was slow.

My second success was with cuttings (prunings, actually) of Huldine, again prepared in December. They were stood in a clear glass of water in a sunny window in our dining room. By the following June, half of them had made roots. Cuttings of so many plants can be rooted in this way, and it is often the only feasible method for gardeners who do not want to be bothered with frames and closed cases.

My failure was with mid-winter cuttings lined out in a specially prepared bed in the open. The place was shady and never allowed to dry out. Although the cuttings never took, I am not convinced that this method need be a flop.

Another fairly simple way in which I, on several occasions, managed to root a small number of cuttings of Lady Betty Balfour, was by taking buds, each with a heel of old wood, in late winter, inserting them in cutting compost round the edge of a $3\frac{1}{2}$-in. pot and keeping them in a closed cold frame.

So much for hole-and-corner methods. I will next describe how I propagate nearly all types of clematis in large quantities from cuttings and then go on to consider what are, perhaps, the more usual commercial practices in this country.

The unusual aspect of my own method is that it is all done without artificial heating—only the sun's heat on cold frames. The Dutch do a lot of propagating this way too and, of course, it does keep overheads down to a minimum. The frames have double walls and double glazing, and are thus able to retain a great deal of the heat absorbed by day, throughout the night. In Holland the cuttings are inserted directly into beds made up in the frames. I do mine into pots, mainly because it is so much more comfortable for a rheumaticky person to work at a potting bench than to grovel about on his hands and knees in a frame.

My stock plants are outside and they have not trails of young growth long enough for propagation until the first week in May, so this is when the job starts, and it is mostly completed by the end of July. A trail is chopped up with secateurs just above each node. After this you can either make one cutting from each node or you can make two. The advantage in the first case is in having a more substantial cutting, and if one bud fails the other may succeed. The procedure here, then, is to trim the internode at 1 to 1½ in. below the node, remove one leaf and, on the same side as the removed leaf, cut away a thin sliver of stem along the whole length of the cutting from just below the bud. This operation is not essential but does encourage rooting from the sides of the cutting as well as from the base. I do not use rooting hormones. I have tried them and found no difference in the results from when they were not used.

The advantage of making two cuttings from each node is, obviously, in the number of plants produced. In this case a longitudinal cut is made, with a razor blade, down the centre of each stem, starting at the node and finishing off with a cross-cut 1 to 1½ in. below. It is very quickly done. Each cutting has its leaf left intact and about eight cuttings are inserted into each 3½-in. pot. Again the compost consists of the John Innes formula: one part sterilised loam, two parts peat and three parts sand—actually grit (usually ground up shingle), since no natural sand is coarse and sharp-draining enough.

The importance of having an intact, undamaged leaf on each cutting should be emphasised. It is astonishing to find it stated in some books on clematis that, to quote one of them: 'Any leaves should, of course, be detached in preparing the cutting.' On the contrary. A soft or half-ripe cutting taken during the growing season is invariably leafy, for it is through its leaf that the cutting synthesises the hormones and carbohydrates necessary for its rooting. The main difficulty with rooting clematis cuttings is when the old foliage rots before roots and a new shoot have been made. Care of the cuttings during their first six weeks is a skilled and exacting task. They must be given as much light as possible, yet not be allowed to get scorched. Their foliage should be moist by day and dry by night when the temperature is falling. This may entail frequent sprinkling of the foliage from about 9 a.m. B.S.T. until 4 p.m., and none thereafter. The frame lights will

32. *C. heracleifolia davidiana*. Pale blue.

33. *C. heracleifolia
davidiana* (close-up).

34. *C.* × *jouiniana*. Off-white,
shading to grey-blue at tips.

need shading. It is a great help to spray the clematis once a week with an organic fungicide like captan as a protection from the Grey Mould fungus, *Botrytis cinerea*, which is Enemy No. 1 in the propagation frame.

Rooting takes place in five or six weeks and the cuttings can then be hardened off a little, prior to potting them up. They can, if strong, go straight into their final pots and these are set out in ordinary cold frames, kept closed and well shaded until the young plants are established. When thoroughly hardened off they are lined out in plunge beds, each plant with its cane.

The use of heated glass and propagation under mist very materially speeds up the whole operation and extends the propagating season so that it can go forward continuously from early March to September. The cuttings are inserted into seed trays which stand on the heated bench, but full ventilation is maintained by day in the mist house. The cuttings root in a fortnight to six weeks and are potted off into thumb pots. Weaning and hardening off after rooting under mist is a gradual process, the young plants being kept in closed frames in a section of the house where the mist units are not operating, and ventilation is gradually introduced. They are then given their final potting and lined out in a cold house, at first kept closed but gradually being given increasing ventilation.

For the professional, it is simplest to organise propagation so that as many clematis species and varieties as possible are given similar treatment. But the amateur who finds the striking of large-flowered hybrids a bit beyond him can still be successful with easy species like *C. macropetala* and the *montana* group. They can be rooted in an ordinary cold frame at any time from May to September. The *montana* group are easily rooted in spring, before they have started making trails of growth, by detaching a half-node (from an old stem) consisting of one main leaf, a leafy axillary bud and a heel of old wood. This comprises the cutting. Its heel is trimmed and it is then treated in the usual manner.

Clematis armandii seems to root best from cuttings of fairly ripe wood of the current season taken between September and November. Potting off of the rooted cuttings can quite well be delayed till the following spring. While there is no difficulty about rooting this species, its bud rather frequently fails to break dormancy and make a shoot.

LAYERING

The most satisfactory way to get an extra plant or two of a large-flowered clematis growing in your or in a friend's garden, is by layering it. By this method, a very strong plant is obtained in a matter of only nine months.

The most common error, when layering is attempted, is to use shoots of the current season's growth. These will always die without making roots. The stretch used should be at least two seasons, i.e., eighteen months, old. Indeed, the older the stem the better it roots. Clematis must be rather exceptional in this respect.

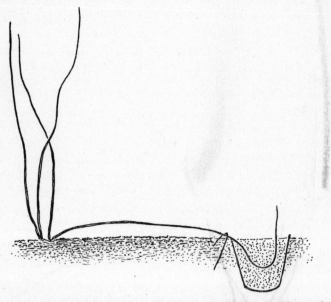

FIG. 4. LAYERING CLEMATIS. This is an excellent way of increasing one's stock of large-flowered clematis under garden conditions. The shoots layered should be at least two seasons old. Root the layer in a 6- or 7-in. pot filled with cutting compost and insert the stem to about two-thirds of the pot's depth, holding it firm with a peg. When the stem is in position, firm the compost well. In autumn, the layer, which by now should be well rooted, is severed from the parent plant.

The job can be done at any convenient time during the dormant season and up till the end of March. First a 6-in. or 7-in. pot is plunged to its rim in a convenient spot. It is filled with cutting compost (see p. 84) and a portion of the selected stem is pushed into it to about two-thirds of the pot's depth. The curve which the stem describes should be made as angular as possible without actually kinking it. At the point just before the stem enters the pot, its position is fixed by pushing a wooden peg into the ground. Where the stem emerges from the pot, it can be severed above a node so as to leave about 6 in. of old stem. But if long enough it need not be severed at all but can be layered into a second pot, perhaps even into a third, thus describing a sea-serpentine course. Once the stem's position has been fixed in the pot, the cutting compost should be well firmed. The pots will need watering during dry spells in the summer. In autumn, when growth has ceased, the layer is severed from the parent stem and the pot should be full of roots, ready for transplanting.

DIVISION

Herbaceous clematis like *C. recta*, *C. heracleifolia* var. *davidiana* and *C. integrifolia* can be propagated in the dormant season by simple division.

If you have to lift an old specimen of a large-flowered hybrid clematis, you will often find that it has a number of stems arising from below ground level (sometimes as many as ten or twelve, with Nelly Moser) and that these can all be cut apart so as to leave roots on each of them, thus constituting new plants ready made.

SEED

Raising clematis from seed is fun but, unless one is intent on the production of new varieties or of stock plants for grafting, it is of only slight importance as a propagating method. *C. tangutica* is an exception. Seed sown in spring germinates in three weeks and plants come on so fast that they may even flower in their first autumn.

Seed of the large-flowered hybrids is slow to germinate. Sown in the autumn of ripening, they may start to germinate by the following June but can take anything up to three years, and germination is very uneven. The resulting plants are unlikely to be as good as the seed parent.

Self-sown seedlings will often turn up in the garden, particularly of *C. montana*, *C. tangutica* and *C. flammula*, but even of the hybrid types, on occasions. *C. recta* seeds itself like a weed.

Part 2

Descriptive List
of Clematis in Cultivation

In this section I have aimed at giving each clematis a sufficiently detailed description for the reader to be able to check up on the identity, correct or otherwise, of any cultivated clematis that may come his way. This has been my aim, but I am well aware that it has not always been fulfilled. I own a large collection of clematis, but by no means all. My friends (especially John Treasure) have been most helpful in filling lacunae, but even so the details I would have liked are sometimes missing. Some of my data is derived from clematis grown in pots, but their performance is not in these circumstances characteristic of their performance in the garden. I have not yet managed to find places for them all in my garden, for clematis are no monomania with me and I like to grow a very wide range of plants.

Following the name of each species or variety will be found the letter A, B or C. This refers to the method of pruning required (related, as it is, to the season of flowering) and the key is given on page 68 in the chapter on pruning.

After this I have tried to include the following details: vigour; number of leaflets into which the leaf is subdivided; size of flower; number and shape of sepals; their colour; colour of the stamens (or anthers); season of flowering. Other distinguishing features are included when they seem useful. Country of origin and date of introduction (when known) are given for species described.

Size of flower is the trickiest character, where I have not been able to refer it to a garden specimen. It is likely to be little more than half-size on a young pot-plant, but allowance has been made for this fact in the sizes quoted.

89

Abundance (C). Vigorous. Leaflets, five, and further subdivided. Flowers semi-nodding, 2 in. across. Sepals, four or five, light red with darker veins. Stamens creamy. June-August.

C. afoliata (syn. *C. aphylla*) (A). New Zealand. Introduced 1908. Climber to 8 ft. or more, Evergreen in a special sense; no true foliage, the leaf being reduced to a tendril. Stems rush-like, green, becoming yellowish in winter. Flowers in clusters of two, three or four, nodding, ¾ to 1 in. across at mouth. Sepals, normally four, 1¼ in. long, obliquely spreading, pale-straw-coloured with green undertone. April-May. Dioecious. Untidy grower but unobtrusively pleasing when in flower. Needs a warm wall.

Alba Luxurians (C). Vigorous, allied to *C. viticella*. Leaflets, seven, further subdivided. Flowers 3½ in. across. Sepals, four, white, with green, recurved tips. Pronounced eye of dark stamens. June-September.

C. alpina (syn. *Atragene alpina*) (A). Central and southern Europe to north-east Asia. 1792. Deciduous climber to 10 ft. Flowers nodding. Sepals, four, 1 to 1½ in. long. Whitish petaloid stamens. April-May. The variety *sibirica*, introduced from Siberia 1753, has yellowish-white flowers. For named cultivars of these two see under Columbine, Pamela Jackman, Ruby and White Moth. All are liable to carry a light second crop in late summer.

C. armandii (A). China. 1900. Vigorous evergreen climber to 20 ft., but requiring wall protection. Leaves ternate, large and tough; coppery when young. Flowers 2 in. wide in dense axillary clusters. Delightful scent. Sepals, five or six, white. Stamens creamy. April-May. Snowdrift is a selection with the largest, whitest blossoms. Apple Blossom is faintly tinged with pink while opening.

C. × aromatica (syn. *C. coeruleo-odorata*) (C). (*C. flammula × C. integrifolia*) circa 1845. Herbaceous, non-clinging, to 6 ft. Leaves sometimes simple, ovate or irregularly lobed; sometimes compound, with 3 or 5 leaflets. Panicles of 1½ in. wide, violet-blue flowers with white stamens. Scented. July-September.

Ascotiensis (C). Vigorous. Leaves simple or ternate. Flowers 5 in. across. Sepals, four, five or six, ovate, 2 in. wide. Bright lavender-blue. Stamens greenish. July-September.

Barbara Dibley (B). Moderately vigorous. Leaves ternate. Flowers 6 to 7½ in. across. Sepals, eight, long, narrow and fine pointed. Sumptuous petunia red throughout. Fades badly. Anthers reddish-purple. May-June.

Barbara Jackman (B). Moderately vigorous. Leaves ternate. Flowers

up to 6 in. across. Sepals, eight, broad, overlapping, tapering briskly
to sharp points. Bluish-purple with vivid magenta bar, at first; fades to
pale mauve but central bar remains crimson. Contrasting eye of creamy
stamens. May-June.

Beauty of Richmond (B). Vigour moderate. Leaves simple or ternate.
Flowers 6 in. or more across. Sepal, six, rosy-blue. Anthers creamy.
May-June.

Beauty of Worcester (B). Moderate vigour. Leaves simple or ternate.
Double flowers on old wood; single on young. Sepals then six, straight
edged, overlapping, tapering to sharp points. Very well formed, solid
flower of rich, deep blue with slight reddish flush at centre base of
sepals. Distinct creamy stamens, with tinge of green. May-September.

Bees' Jubilee (B). Weakly. Leaves trifoliate. Flowers 6 to 7 in. across.
Sepals, usually eight. Colouring as for Nelly Moser but more intense
and vivid. May-June.

Belle Nantaise (C). Moderate vigour. Leaves simple or ternate.
Flowers 8 to 9 in. across. Sepals, six or seven, tapering to acute points.
Pale lavender with whitish stamens. July-October.

Belle of Woking (B). Only moderately vigorous. Leaves simple, broad
and rounded. Flowers very double, 6 in. across, silvery-mauve and most
attractive. May-June.

Blue Belle (C). The plant sold under this name has frequently been
Etoile Violette. I have not seen the true Blue Belle, although it does
exist. Flowers less regular in outline and blacker toned than Etoile
Violette, with a shorter season. August.

Blue Gem (B). Vigorous. Leaves simple or ternate. Flowers only 5 in.
across, well shaped. Sepals, six or seven, broad and overlapping, pale
blue with darker veins, fading to off-white. Rougher textured than Mrs
Bush. Prominent purple anthers. May-June, August-September.

Bracebridge Star (B). Weakish, Leaflets, three, widely separated on
long sub-petioles. Flowers 5 in. across. Sepals, eight, narrowish, inclined
to be gappy. Mauve with deeper rosy-mauve bar. Anthers rosy-mauve.

C. calycina (syn. *C. balearica*) (A). Southern Europe. 1783. Evergreen
climber to 15 ft. with deeply toothed, ternate leaves giving fern-like
effect. Foliage turns to bronzy-purple in cold weather but may get
entirely frosted in severe winters. Flowers nodding, 1½ in. across. Sepals,
four, greenish-yellow with reddish-brown spots. Elusively fragrant under
favourable conditions. January-April. Good on a sheltered north wall.

C. campaniflora (C). Portugal, 1820. Vigorous, climbing to 15 ft.

Leaflets, five, seven or nine, subdivided into threes. Small, 1-in.-wide bells. Sepals, four, bluish-white. July-August.

Campanile. See *C. heracleifolia*.

C. chrysocoma (A). Yunnan. 1890, approx. Shrub to 8 ft. or climber to 30 ft. (two forms). Leaves trifoliate, purplish when young, covered with down. Flowers in axillary clusters of three to five, 2½ in. across, on extra long, 3 to 4 in., downy stalks. Sepals, four, broad and rounded, soft pinkish-mauve. May. Often a second crop August-September, with flowers borne singly from axils of young shoots.

C. cirrhosa (A). Southern Europe, Asia Minor, 1596. Evergreen climber to 10 ft. Leaves simple, ovate or three-lobed with serrated margins. Flowers nodding, 1½ in. across, Sepals, four, whitish. January-May. Closely related to *C. calycina* and requiring similar protection.

C. columbiana. See *C. verticillaris*.

Columbine (A). A selection of *C. alpina* (q.v.). Flowers 3 in. across when wide open, but sepals usually obliquely spreading. Light blue. Staminodes white. April-May.

Comtesse de Bouchaud (C). Very vigorous and free. Leaflets usually five. Flowers 5 to 6 in. across at start of season, smaller later. Sepals, six, markedly channelled along midribs, margins and tips recurved on opening but becoming incurved with age. Bright pinky-mauve. Stamens cream. Mid-June to August.

Côte d'Azur. See *C. heracleifolia*.

Countess of Lovelace (B). Tricky to start but vigorous when established. Leaves ternate. Flowers 5 in. across packed with approximately 70 narrow, pointed sepals. Lilac-blue, fading. Stamens whitish. Carpels form a greenish eye. May-June. Light crop of single blooms later.

Countess of Onslow (C). Semi-woody climber to 15 ft. related to *C. texensis*. Leaflets, three or five. Bell flowers 1½ in. long by 1½ in. wide at mouth. Sepals, four, with pale pink margins deepening to cerise centre on both surfaces, but colour transition more marked on outside of bell. July-October.

Crimson King (B). Rather weak grower. Leaves simple or ternate. Flowers up to 5 in. across. Sepals, five, six or seven, rather gappy and recurving along margins with age. Fairly uniform but tired crimson lake. Filaments white, anthers markedly brown.

C. crispa (C). South-eastern United States, 1726. Semi-woody climber to 4 ft. Leaflets three, five or more. Flowers solitary, bell-shaped, 1½ to 2 in. long, scented. Sepals, four, purplish, with recurved points. July-August. Related to *C. texensis* with which it has been crossed.

35. *C. alpina* Columbine (light blue) on a *Cotoneaster horizontalis*.

36. *C. armandii* Snowdrift. White.

C. W. Dowman (B). New. Resembles Nelly Moser but much pinker. Sepals, eight. Pale stamens.

Daniel Deronda (B). Moderate vigour. Leaves simple or ternate, bronzed. Flowers semi-double, flattish, 7 in. across in May-June; bluish-purple. Single flowers July-August, with paler centre to sepals. Cream stamens.

C. davidiana. See *C. heracleifolia.*

Duchess of Albany (C). Herbaceous or semi-woody climber to 10 ft., related to *C. texensis.* Leaflets, five. 1½-in.-long bell flowers. Sepals, four, clear pink. July-September.

Duchess of Edinburgh (B). Weakish. Leaves ternate, a yellowish-green. Flowers double, white rosettes, 5 in. across, but often misshapen and green, probably due to virus infection. Stamens creamy. May-June.

Duchess of Sutherland (B or C). Sometimes difficult to start but vigorous when happy and established. Leaves ternate. Light pruning allows small crop of flattish double flowers, 6 in. across, early summer. Main crop August-September. Sepals, six, very broad and widely overlapping, tapering to sharp right-angular points. Intense crimson-red. Filaments creamy, anthers reddish-purple. In the other form of Duchess of Sutherland, the sepals have a lighter central bar.

Durandii (Jackmanii × *C. integrifolia*) (C). Sub-shrub to 8 ft. dying back to 1 or 2 ft. from the base in winter. Simple, ovate, non-clinging foliage. Flowers 4 in. across, rich indigo blue. Sepals, four, five or six, with deeply furrowed midribs. Stamens off-white. Late June-September.

Edouard Desfossé (B). Fairly vigorous. Leaves simple or ternate. Flowers 7 in. across. Sepals, eight, long, rather gappy; deep mauve-purple, fading. Reddish-purple central bar. Very conspicuous reddish-purple anthers.

Edward Prichard (C). Herbaceous, 4 to 5 ft. tall, non-clinging. Leaflets, five, deeply toothed. Flowers in terminal and axillary panicles, cruciform, 1½ in. across. Sepals narrow, wedge shaped, pale mauve, deepest near their blunt tips. Picks well, its pleasant scent filling a room. From a cross between *C. recta* and *C. heracleifolia* var. *davidiana.*

Elsa Späth (B). Moderate vigour. Leaflets, three or five. Very large, floppy flowers, 8 in. across. Sepals, six, seven or eight, broad and overlapping, rich lavender-blue. Anthers reddish purple. May-June and again later.

C. × *eriostemon* (syn. *C. bergeronii, C. chandleri, C.* × *intermedia, C. hendersonii*) (C). Introduced 1835. A cross between *C. viticella* and *C. integrifolia* made at different times in different places. Hence the many synonyms. Herbaceous, non-clinging to 8 ft. Leaflets up to seven. Nodding, lantern flowers up to 2 in. across, very like *C. integrifolia*. Sepals, four, dusky purple. Prolific. July-Sept.

Ernest Markham (B or C). Vigorous to 12 ft. Leaflets, three or (usually) five. Light pruning (B) allows preliminary small crop of large flowers, 6 in. across, early June. Main crop always on young shoots; flowers 5 in. across. Sepals, six, broad, overlapping, rough textured, bright magenta. Stamens beige, inconspicuous. July-September.

Etoile de Paris (B). Fairly vigorous. Leaves trifoliate, small, dark and leathery. Flowers 6½ in. across. Sepals, eight, fine pointed, gappy, strong mauve-blue with reddish central bar. Anthers dusty, greyish-purple. May-June.

Etoile Rose (C). Herbaceous climber to 12 ft., related to *C. texensis*. Nodding bell flowers, 2 in. long by 2 in. wide at mouth. Sepals, four, silvery-pink at margins, cherry-purple centred. July-September.

Etoile Violette (C). Vigorous. Leaflets, five. Deep purple, cream-eyed, 4-in.-wide flowers. Sepals, six (sometimes four or five), recurved at tips. July-September.

Fair Rosamond (B). Vigour moderate. Leaflets, three or five. Fat globular buds opening to full, well-formed flower, 5 to 6 in. across. Sepals, eight, broad and overlapping. White with network of pink veins. Prominent cushion of bright purple anthers very conspicuous. Sweet but not sickly scent. May-June.

Fairy Queen (B). Rather weak growing. Leaflets, three. Flowers 7 in. or more across. Sepals, eight, 1½ in. across, a little gappy. Flesh coloured with rosy-mauve bar. Anthers dusty purple. May-June.

C. fargesii (C). China, 1911. Vigorous. Leaflets, seven, widely spaced. Flowers in compound panicles, white, 1½ in. across, saucer shaped. Sepals, six or seven, blunt, notched at tip, obovate, ⅔ in. across. Stamens greenish. June-September.

C. flammula (C). Southern Europe, 1590. Vigorous, to 15 ft. Foliage rich, dark green. Leaves biternate. Thousands of inch-wide, pure white cruciform blossoms, powerfully scented. August-October.

C. florida bicolor (syn. *C. sieboldii*) (B). Not vigorous but capable of reaching 8 ft. Hardy, though early spring growth often cut. Leaflets, five. Flowers borne singly in leaf axils of terminal 3 ft. of young growth. Peduncles 8 in. long with conspicuous foliar bracts. Flowers 4 in. across. Sepals, six, ovate, 1½ in. across; pale green, slowly expanding and maturing to white. Anthers petal-like, massed in a domed boss, eventually 2 in. across, changing from green to rich purple and persisting for some time after the sepals have fallen. June-late August.

The most surprising of all clematis. *C. florida bicolor* is often mistaken for a Passion Flower but is really far more effective. Likes a sunny aspect with generous feeding and watering.

C. fusca (C). North-east Asia, 1860. Herbaceous or semi-woody climber to 12 ft. Leaves pinnate, the terminal leaflet often absent. Flowers solitary, urn-shaped. Sepals, four, $\frac{3}{4}$-1 in. long with recurved tips, reddish-brown outside. July-August. Inconspicuous, but interesting as an Asiatic relative of the mainly North American Viorna group, including *C. texensis*, *C. viorna*, *C. pitcherii* and *C. crispa*.

Gipsy Queen (C). Vigorous. Leaves ternate. Flowers 5 in. across. Sepals, six, broad and rounded, purple fading to violet. Anthers reddish-purple. June-August.

Gravetye Beauty (C). Vigorous herbaceous climber allied to *C. texensis*. Leaflets, five, often heart shaped. $2\frac{3}{4}$-in.-long bells open out into $3\frac{1}{2}$-in.-wide stars. Sepals, four, five or six, with incurved margins but recurved tips. Cherry-red, ageing pinker. Filaments cream, anthers same cherry-red as sepals. July-October.

Guiding Star (B). Fairly vigorous. Leaflets, three or five. Flowers 5 in. across. Sepals, six, seven or eight, stiffly held, tapering to fine points. Gappy. Bluish-purple with reddish-purple streaks. Anthers purple. May-June.

Hagley Hybrid (C). So abundant in flower production for three solid months that growth tends to be limited. Seldom taller than 8 ft. Leaves usually ternate. Flowers 5 to 6 in. across. Sepals, six (or five), cupped, tapering to fine points. A delightful rosy-mauve at first but fading. Handsome purplish anthers. June-September.

Henryi (syn. Bangholme Belle) (B). Vigour moderate once established but young plants often fail. Young foliage characteristically bronzed. Leaves simple or ternate. Flowers 6 to 7 in. across, beautifully shaped. Sepals, six, scarcely overlapping, pure white. Contrasting eye of brown-tipped stamens. Two crops. May-September.

C. heracleifolia (C). Eastern China, 1837. Coarse, non-clinging sub-shrub to 5 ft. Large ternate leaves, the central leaflet twice the size of the other two. Flowers hyacinth-like in size and shape, borne in axillary clusters and whorls. Sepals, four (five or six), blue. July-September. Best known in gardens in three named cultivars and one natural variety:

davidiana, Northern China, 1864. 3 ft., herbaceous. Flowers dioecious (usually male in cultivation), pale blue, larger and opening wider ($1\frac{1}{2}$ in.

across) than normal. Very fragrant. Wyevale is a slightly deeper shaded form with markedly larger flowers and as good a scent.

Campanile. sub-shrub to 4 ft. Hermaphrodite. Numerous, ¾-in.-long, mid-blue bell-flowers. **Côte d'Azur,** similar but a slightly deeper blue.

Horace Young (B). New. Mid-blue, nicely shaped flower. Sepals, eight, widely overlapping. Stamens white.

Huldine (C). Vigorous. Leaflets, five. Flowers 4 in. across. Sepals, usually six, not overlapping, with slightly incurved margins but recurved tips. Upper surface white; under surface pale mauve, with darker central bar. Stamens greenish-white. July-September.

Hybrida Sieboldii (syn. 'Ramona', in America) (B). A large, lavender-blue clematis, with which I am not personally familiar, but very close to Blue Gem, Mrs Bush and Mrs Hope.

C. indivisa (A). New Zealand, 1840. Evergreen climber with trifoliate leaves. Flowers 2 to 3 in. across, unisexual, the slightly larger males most often in cultivation. Sepals, six to eight, spathulate, pure white. Stamens yellow. April-May. For a warm, sheltered wall or cool greenhouse. The variety *lobata* has toothed leaflets.

C. integrifolia (C). Southern Europe, 1573. Herbaceous to 4 ft. Leaves simple, ovate with three grooved longitudinal veins; non-clinging. Flowers nodding, 2 in. across. Sepals, four, obliquely spreading, mid-blue on both surfaces, their margins recurved and somewhat twisted. Stamens white, forming a tube. July-September; the variety *hendersonii* is larger.

Jackmanii (C). Vigorous. Leaves simple (at base of young shoots), ternate (along middle of young shoots) or in fives (towards extremities of young shoots). Flowers 5 in. across. Sepals, four (five and six), gappy, rough-textured with channelled mid-ribs. Bluish-purple. Stamens greenish-beige. July-August.

Jackmanii alba (B or C). Very vigorous with pale green foliage. Leaflets, three. First crop of flowers, 5 in. across, semi-double, of ragged appearance with sepals of unequal lengths and often undecided whether to be leaves, on the outside, or stamens, in the middle of the flower. White with pale blue veins. Second crop of flowers 5 in. across, single. Sepals, five or six, white. Anthers brown. May-June and August-September. Hard pruning (C) will eliminate first crop.

Jackmanii rubra (B). Fairly vigorous. Leaves ternate. Flowers, semi-double from year-old wood, slightly lopsided. Second crop single. Sepals, four, five or six, velvety crimson-lake. Cream stamens. May-September.

37. TAKING CUTTINGS

(*a*) Cutting up a trail of young growth above each node.

(*b*) Dividing a stem longitudinally to get two cuttings from one node.

(c) Inserting the cuttings round the edge of a pot, avoiding overlapping foliage.

(d) Cold frame with double walls and glazing. Cuttings sprayed with captan.

Jackmanii superba (C). Very vigorous and prolific, differing from Jackmanii only in its broader sepals composing a fuller flower and having a reddish tinge in its purple colouring. July-September.

C. × *jouiniana* (*C. heracleifolia* var. *davidiana* × *C. vitalba*) (C). Non-clinging sub-shrub to 12 ft. or more. Leaves dark green, glabrous; leaflets, five (or three). Huge, compound, leafy panicles of wide-opening flowers 1 to 2 in. across. Sepals, four, five or six, off-white shading to grey-blue at tips. Stamens cream. Late August-October. The variety *praecox* flowers a month to six weeks earlier.

Kathleen Dunford (B). New. Large, semi-double, with two symmetrical rows of fairly narrow sepals. A rather dim magenta. Anthers brown. May-June with some single flowers later.

Kermesina (C). Of medium vigour with small, wine-red flowers like those of *C. viticella*. See p. 49.

King Edward VII (B). Fairly vigorous. Leaves simple or ternate. Flowers 6 in. or more across. Sepals, eight, broadly ovate, widely overlapping. Lilac-mauve but with bluer margins. Handsome and distinct. Anthers dusty lilac. May-June.

King George V (C). Vigour moderate. Leaves ternate. Flowers 6 in. across. Sepals, six or seven, flesh pink with bright pink bar. July-September.

Lady Betty Balfour (C). Vigorous to 12 ft. or more. Leaves ternate (sometimes one or five), shiny, coppery when young. Flowers 5 in. across. Sepals, six, rather cupped, fine-pointed. Rich purple fading to bluer shade. White central bar on underside. Stamens creamy, conspicuous. September. Needs full sun.

Lady Caroline Nevill (B). Fairly vigorous. Leaves simple or ternate. Flowers 6 or 7 in. across. Sepals, eight, fairly pale lavender with very faintly darker midrib. Filaments white, anthers beige. May-June; August-September. Sometimes semi-double in first flush.

Lady Londesborough (B). Growth moderate. Leaves ternate. Flowers 5 to 6 in. across, beautifully formed. Sepals, seven, broad, round-tipped with wide overlap. Pale mauve, fading to silvery-mauve and finally palest grey. Prominent dark stamens. May-June.

Lady Northcliffe (B). Fairly vigorous if it can be established. Slight coppery tinge in young leaves. Leaflets, one, three or five. Flowers 6 in. across. Sepals, usually six, broadly overlapping, wavy and never lying flat, much blunter than Lasurstern. Deep, slightly richer blue than Lasurstern. Stamens greenish-white, less prominent than those of Lasurstern. May-June, August-September.

G

Lagoon (A). A selection of *C. macropetala* (q.v.) with the typical lavender colouring.

Lasurstern (B). Fairly vigorous, to 9 ft. Leaves sometimes simple, usually ternate. Flowers 6 to 7 in. wide, opening perfectly flat. Sepals, seven or eight with wavy margins (cf. Lady Northcliffe in which entire sepal is twisted), tapering to fine points. Rich, deep blue fading to campanula blue. Greenish-white bar on under-surface. Stamens pale creamy. May-June and August-September. Second crop flowers only 5 in. across.

Lawsoniana (C). Moderate vigour. Leaves simple or ternate. Flowers 9 in. across. Sepals, six, broad, overlapping slightly; purplish-blue with rosy tint. Stamens pale fawn. Not known to me personally although a very old variety. Probably flowers midsummer onwards.

Lincoln Star (B). Not much vigour. Leaves ternate. Flowers 5 in. across, the eight narrow, pointed sepals composing a shapely star. Brilliant raspberry-pink almost to margins, though sometimes this colour is confined to a central bar and autumn blooms may be quite wishy-washy. Anthers crimson and showy. May-June and a scattering in autumn.

Little Nell (C). Vigorous climber to 20 ft. Leaflets five or seven and further subdivided. Flowers $2\frac{1}{2}$ in. across on 5 in. pedicels. Sepals, four or six, recurved at margins. Broad outer band of pale mauve; white central bar. Stamens greenish. July-September.

Lord Nevill (B). Vigorous. Leaves simple or ternate, deeply bronzed when young. Flowers 6 to 7 in. across. Sepals eight (sometimes six), broad and overlapping, giving slightly double effect; very wavy edged, tapering broadly to sharp points. Purplish-blue, especially purple towards centre-base. Veins conspicuously darker throughout the sepal and especially as the flower bleaches. Purple anthers form no contrast. May-June, August-September.

Lucie Lemoine (B). Weakly. Leaflets, three. Flowers, double, white, similar to those of Duchess of Edinburgh; probably identical, as found today.

C. macropetala (syn. *Atragene macropetala*) (A). Northern China, Siberia, 1910. Vigorous climber to 15 ft. Leaves biternate, serrate. Flowers nodding, 3 in. across, conspicuously and fully double. Sepals, four, $1\frac{1}{2}$ in. long by $\frac{3}{4}$ in. wide, lavender with blue margins. Numerous slender staminodes, $1\frac{1}{4}$ in. long; the outer 10 to 14 blue, the inner ones whitish. April-May and a scattering in autumn. For cultivars, see Lagoon, Maidwell Hall, Markham's Pink (syn. Markhamii).

Mme Baron-Veillard (C). Vigorous, to 15 ft. in a season. Leaves ternate, each leaflet on a long stalk. Flowers rather cupped at centre but with slightly reflexed tips, 5 in. across. Sepals, six, obovate, slightly gappy, a nice rosy-lilac shade. Stamens greenish-white. August-October.

Mme Edouard André (C). Not vigorous but nevertheless quite a good doer; to 9 ft. Leaves simple or ternate. Buds narrow, pointed. Flowers up to 5 in. across, rather cupped. Sepals, six, very pointed; margins incurved (cf. Ville de Lyon). Uniformly deep wine red, matt surfaced. Stamens creamy. June-August.

Mme Grangé (C). Vigorous, but may start late into growth after a hard winter. Leaflets, five. Flowers 5 in. across, freely borne. Sepals, four, five or (usually) six; inrolled margins most pronounced on young plants. Upper surface deep purplish-red, velvety. Lower surface pubescent, dusky. Stamens grubby, nondescript. July-August.

Mme Jules Corrévon (C). Vigorous. Leaflets, five, further subdivided. Flowers 5 in. across. Sepals, four, five or six, narrow and gappy with recurved tips, the upper surface deeply channelled. Very good rosy-red. Stamens greenish-cream. Late June-September (long season).

Mme Le Coultre *see* Marie Boisselot.

Maidwell Hall (A). A bluer form of *C. macropetala* (q.v.).

Marcel Moser (B). Rather weak growing, tending to flower at the expense of young growth. Leaves ternate, pubescent when young, longer and more narrowly tapering than those of Nelly Moser. Flowers 8 in. across. Sepals eight, tapering to fine points. Rosy-mauve with carmine central bar. Bleaches badly. Handsome reddish-purple stamens. May-June.

Margot Koster (C). Robust and prolific *viticella*-type clematis. Leaflets, five. Flowers 3 in. across. Sepals, four, five or six, obovate, gappy with reflexed margins and tips. Rosy-red. Stamens whitish. Late June-August.

Marie Boisselot (syn. Mme Le Coultre) (B). Vigorous. Leaves simple or ternate, very broad. Flowers 7 in. across, beautifully formed, opening flat. Sepals, eight, very broad, overlapping so widely as sometimes to give semi-double impression. Faint pink flush at unfolding, but quickly changing to pure white. Stamens white. May-June and again, freely, September-October.

Markham's Pink (syn. *C. macropetala* var. *markhamii*) (A). Similar to *C. macropetala* (q.v.) apart from its colour. Upper surface of sepals bright reddish-purple with narrow pale lilac margin. Inner, concealed staminodes, greenish-cream.

Maureen (?C). Sepals, six, reddish-purple, though bluer toned than Mme Grangé. June-July. I have never seen this clematis.

Minuet (C). Vigorous. Leaflets up to seven, and further subdivided. Nodding, *viticella*-like flowers on long pedicels, each with two foliar bracts. Sepals, four, margined in deep mauve (pale purple), the inner area off-white with mauve veins. Stamens green. July-August.

Miriam Markham (B). Rather weak growing. Large, loosely built double flowers, shaded lavender. May-June. Occasional single blooms later.

Miss Bateman (B). Fairly vigorous. Leaves ternate. Flowers 6 in. across, opening flat and well formed. Sepals, eight, broad, overlapping, creamy-white. Reddish-purple anthers make a striking eye. May-June.

Miss Crawshay (B). Vigour moderate. Leaves ternate. Buds very fat, opening into (usually) semi-double blooms, 6 in. across. Single blooms have eight sepals, round-tipped, narrow at base. Delightful pale rosy-mauve. Anthers pale fawn. May-June.

Mrs Bush (B). Fairly vigorous. Leaves ternate. Flowers 6 to 7 in. across or more. Sepals, eight, very soft, silky texture, fairly (but not too) narrow. Uniformly pale blue. Anthers pale brown. May-June. Compare Blue Gem.

Mrs Cholmondeley (B). Vigorous. Leaflets, three or five. Flowers 8 in. across, prolific. Sepals usually six, obovate, narrow at base and with gaps between sepals. Lavender-blue with darker reticulations in veins. Fades pleasantly. Stamens brownish. May-September. Blowsy old variety but makes a splendid show.

Mrs George Jackman (B). Reasonably vigorous. Leaves simple or (more often) ternate. Flowers 6 to 7 in. across with (usually) eight broad overlapping sepals and sometimes an extra two or three, giving slightly doubled effect. White. Anthers pale beige forming a more conspicuous eye than Marie Boisselot but less so than Henryi and Miss Bateman. May-June and again later.

Mrs Hope (B). Vigorous. Leaves nearly all simple, up to 8 in. long and 4 in. broad in mature plants. Flowers 7 in. across at first flowering, 5 in. at second. Sepals, eight, very broad ($2\frac{1}{4}$ in. across) and so overlapping as to look semi-double—a beautiful shape. Light blue with slightly darker central bar. Anthers rich purple. May-June, August-September.

Mrs N. Thompson (B). New. Like a very dark Barbara Jackman. Sepals six, overlapping. Petunia central bar with bluish-purple margins. Stamens reddish.

Mrs Oud (?B). Weak grower. Leaves ternate. Large white flowers, well shaped. Sepals broad and overlapping. Dark anthers. June. I have failed to establish this.

Mrs P. B. Truax (B). Fairly vigorous. Leaves ternate. Flowers $5\frac{1}{2}$ in. wide. Sepals, usually eight, not much overlapping, very narrow at base, where gaps appear. Mid to light blue, fading. Stamens creamy. May-June. Rather a short season. Has been sold as Xerxes.

Mrs Spencer Castle (B). Vigour moderate. Leaves ternate. Large, pale mauve-pink flowers with cream anthers. Sepals, usually six, but extra ones at first flowering, giving semi-double effect. May-June and again later.

Mrs Wasscher (B). New. Flowers very large and clumsy, 8 in. across. Sepals, seven or eight, broad, mid-lavender with darker bar. Anthers muddy.

C. montana (A). Himalaya, 1831. Exceptionally vigorous, to 30 ft. Leaves ternate with serrated margins. Flowers in axillary clusters up to five, 2 to $2\frac{1}{2}$ in. across, vanilla scented. Sepals, usually four, white. May. The variety *grandiflora* has flowers up to 3 in. across. No scent.

C. montana rubens (A). China, 1900. Leaves purplish, especially when young. Flowers rosy-mauve, 2 to 3 in. across, vanilla scented. May. The following cultivars are in commerce:

ELIZABETH: Large, light pinkish flowers, sometimes white in a young plant's first season. Scented. May.

PICTON'S VARIETY. Substantial flowers. Sepals, four, five or six, of varying widths. Opens deep rosy-mauve, fading only a little. Anthers whitish. Scent negligible.

PINK PERFECTION. Very like Elizabeth.

TETRAROSE. Large rosy-mauve cultivar.

C. montana wilsonii (A). Late flowering, its scented, 3-in. white blooms appearing June-July. Often sold untrue to name.

C. napaulensis (syn. *C. forrestii*) (A). Northern India, China, 1912. Vigorous evergreen climber to 30 ft. Leaves and flowers in axillary clusters. Leaflets, three or five. Flowers, nodding. Sepals, four, $\frac{2}{3}$ in. long, greenish-white. Stamens purple, prominent. Winter-spring. Tender. For cool greenhouse.

Nelly Moser (B). Vigorous to 12 ft. Leaves ternate, smooth (cf. Marcel Moser). Flowers $6\frac{1}{2}$ in. across, opening flat. Sepals, eight, fairly blunt tipped, rosy-mauve with carmine bar. Brilliance of this bar varies greatly from plant to plant and from one season to another. Bleaches badly. Anthers reddish-purple. May-June, September-October.

C. orientalis (syn. *C. graveolens*) (C). Asia, 1731. Vigorous to 20 ft. Size and bright yellow colouring of flowers similar to *C. tangutica* but often opening wide to 2 in., though sometimes campanulate. September-October. Outclassed by L. & S. form No. 13342. Tibet. Introduced by Messrs Ludlow and Sherriff, 1947. Leaflets, up to nine and further finely subdivided. Flowers broadly campanulate with very thick, fleshy sepals. Stamens conspicuous, with reddish-purple filaments and white anthers. Late June-October.

Pamela Jackman (A). A recent selection of *C. alpina* (q.v.). Flowers 3 in. across at mouth. Sepals 1¾ in. long, ⅝ in. wide; of generous proportions for this species. Rich, deep azure. Staminodes in a tight cluster, the outer ring bluish, the inner ones creamy. April-May.

C. paniculata (C). Japan, 1860. Vigorous climber to 30 ft. or more. Leaves smooth, dark and glossy; leaflets, three or five. Flowers 1 in. across, borne profusely in axillary panicles. Hawthorn scented. Sepals, four, white. October. Very popular in the United States but apt to flower too late in Britain.

C. pavoliniana (B). China, 1908. Evergreen, Leaves simple or ternate, cordate, tapering to fine points, 3 in. long. Flowers borne singly in axils, 1½ in. across, strongly hawthorn scented. Sepals, four, narrow, white. Stamens and styles white. June. Needs a warm wall.

Percy Lake (B). New. Large flowers. Sepals, seven or eight, washed-out mauve-white; stamens the same. Disappointing.

Percy Picton (B). Rather weak growing. Leaves ternate. Flowers 6 in. across, dished like a saucer. Sepals usually eight (sometimes only six or seven), perfectly ovate, a rich intense mauve. Anthers purple. May-June and some paler, smaller flowers later.

Perle d'Azur (C). Vigorous to 12 ft. Leaflets three or five. Flowers up to 6 in. across but, with recurved tips, appearing less. Sepals, six (occasionally fewer), broadly obovate, 2½ in. across at broadest. Deeply channelled mid-ribs. Light blue with pinkish-mauve flush towards centre-base. Stamens pale greenish. Late June-August. Very free and striking.

C. pitcherii (syn. *C. simsii*) (C). United States of America, 1878. Climber to 12 ft. Leaflets, three, five or seven, further subdivided. Flowers solitary, urn-shaped. Sepals, four, purplish outside, 1 in. long with recurved tips. July-September. Related to *C. texensis* with which it has been hybridised.

President (syn. The President) (B). Vigorous. Leaves simple or ternate; young foliage bronzed. Flowers up to 7 in. across, somewhat cupped and often showing undersurface. Sepals, eight, overlapping with tapered points. Upper surface uniform light purple; lower surface pale with silvery-white central bar. Anthers reddish-purple. May-October, two or three flushes.

Prins Hendrik (syn. Prince Henry) (B). Weakish growing, but enormous flowered. Leaves usually simple. Sepals, seven, broad, with crimped, wavy margins and fine points; lavender-blue. Anthers purple. Best under glass.

Proteus (B). Moderate vigour. Leaves trifoliate. Buds globular. Flowers fully double at first; pompom rosettes, 6 in. across. Sepals, about 100, rosy-lilac. Second crop of flowers single. Sepals, six, darkest at margins. Stamens cream. May-June; August-October. A fine old variety.

C. recta. Southern and eastern Europe; Northern Asia, 1597. Herbaceous climber. Height variable, 3 to 7 ft. Handsome, deep green pinnate foliage; leaflets, five. Flowers in panicles, white, $\frac{3}{4}$ in. wide, cruciform, heavily scented. June-July. Decorative seed heads. The variety *flore pleno*, double flowered; *purpurea*, young foliage purple, maturing to green.

C. rehderiana (syn. *C. nutans; C. nutans thyrsoidea*) (C). Western China, 1898. Vigorous climber to 20 ft. Leaves and shoots downy; leaflets, seven or nine, coarsely toothed. Flowers in axillary panicles, bell shaped, $\frac{1}{2}$ to $\frac{3}{4}$ in. long. Sepals, four, recurved at tips, straw yellow. Strongly cowslip scented. August-October.

Royal Velours (C). Vigour moderate. Leaflets, five, and further subdivided. Flowers 3 in. across. Sepals, usually four, dark rich reddish-purple, of velvety texture. July-August. I have not seen the real plant, but *viticella rubra* has often been sold as this.

C. × *rubro-marginata* (*C. flammula* × *C. viticella*) (C). Vigorous climber to 12 ft. Flowers 1 in. across. Sepals, four to six, white centred, shading to purple margins. Grubby and ineffective. Scented. August-October.

Ruby (A). A selection of *C. alpina* (q.v.). Flowers up to $3\frac{1}{4}$ in. across. Sepals, $1\frac{1}{2}$ to $1\frac{3}{4}$ in. long, of a dim lilac colouring. Staminodes off-white with mauve tinge. April-May.

C. scottiae (C). Herbaceous, non-clinging, 2 to 3 ft. tall. Leaves glaucous, bipinnate, the leaflets narrow, lanceolate, very attractive. Petioles and underside of leaves downy. Flowers urn-shaped, $1\frac{1}{4}$ in. across, $1\frac{1}{2}$ in. long, the four sepals with recurved tips. Outer surface downy, lavender-coloured, a pinker tinge within. Masses of creamy stamens, slightly protruding. June-July. Easily raised from seed.

Sealand Gem (C). Fairly vigorous. Leaves simple or trifoliate. Flowers 5 to 6 in. across. Sepals, six, perfectly ovate, 1½ in. across. Pale rosy-mauve with carmine bar quickly fading to give uniform colouring. Anthers mauvish, not standing out. Main flowering on young shoots, July-August.

C. serratifolia (C). Korea, 1909. Vigorous woody climber to 12 ft. Leaves biternate. Flowers nodding. Sepals, four, 1-1½ in. long, fairly pale greenish-yellow. Stamens purple. August-October.

Sir Garnet Wolseley (B). Flowers smallish, 4 to 5 in. across. Sepals, seven or eight, a lively lavender throughout; broad white bar on reverse. Filaments white, anthers reddish-purple in striking contrast. The Queen as now seen seems to be identical with this.

Sir Trevor Lawrence (C). Vigorous herbaceous climber allied to *C. texensis*. Leaflets, three, five or seven. Two-inch-long bells with recurved tips. Sepals up to six, very much the same cherry-red colour as Gravetye Beauty but slightly more luminous. Fades to bluer shade. Stamens cream throughout (cf. Gravetye Beauty's red anthers). July-October. Flowers remain urn-shaped.

C. spoonerii (syn. *C. chrysocoma sericea*) (A). China, 1909. Allied to *C. chrysocoma*, climbing to 25 ft. Downy shoots and ternate leaves. Flowers white, 3 in. across, on 4 in. or longer, downy stalks. Sepals, four, broad and round-tipped. May-June.

Star of India (C). Vigour only moderate unless on good soil. Leaflets, three or five, broad and bold. Flowers 5½ to 6½ in. across of excellent shape with four, five or six broadly ovate sepals, up to 2½ in. wide. Purple with broad reddish-purple central bar which gradually fades out. Stamens grubby, nondescript. A handsome and dashing cultivar. July-September.

C. tangutica (C). China, 1898. Vigorous climber to 15 ft. Leaflets up to seven, unevenly toothed, unprepossessing. Flowers campanulate, 1 to 1½ in. long. Sepals, four, butter yellow inside and out. Conspicuous seed heads with feathery styles. Late June-October. The variety *obtusiuscula* and a selection from it, Gravetye Variety, have smaller, deeper yellow flowers. By contrast, Jack Drake's form, collected by him in a Canadian garden 30 years ago, has flowers quite twice as large as normal.

C. uncinata (syn. *C. leiocarpa*) (C). Central China, 1901. Evergreen with pinnate or biternate foliage. Flowers in axillary panicles from current season's growth. About 1½ in. across with four narrow, white sepals. Slight but not agreeable scent. October. Related to the superior species *C. armandii*, and like it requires wall protection. Easily raised from seed.

C. × vedrariensis (*C. chrysocoma* × *C. montana rubens*) (A). Climber to 20 ft. Leaves trifoliate, downy, deeply serrated. Flowers rosy-mauve, 2½-3 in. across on 4 in., downy stalks. Sepals, four, five, or six. May. *C. vedrariensis rosea* (syn. *C. spoonerii rosea*), very similar. Highdown, a good form of the above.

Venosa Violacea (C). Vigorous. Leaflets, five, subdivided into three or five. Viticella-type, but with 4-in. wide, upward facing flowers. Sepals, five or six with purple incurved margins and white, purple-veined centres. Stamens abortive. July-September.

C. verticillaris (syn. *Atragene americana*) (A). North America: Hudson Bay to Utah. 1797. Woody climber to 10 ft. Leaves ternate. Flowers solitary, nodding, 2 to 3 in. wide. Sepals, four, 1½ in. long, purplish-blue as also outer staminodes. May. This is the North American counterpart of *C. macropetala* and *C. alpina*. *C. verticillaris* var. *columbiana* is commoner in cultivation.

Victoria (C). Vigorous. Leaflets, five. Flowers 6 in. across, opening flat, without recurving. Sepals, six, sometimes four or five, with deep central veins and minutely puckered surface, broadly ovate, 2 in. across. Light rosy-purple with more intensely flushed central bar. Fades pleasantly. Buff stamens. July-September.

Ville de Lyon (B). Vigorous to 12 ft. Leaflets, three or five. Flowers in two big crops. Maximum diameter 5 to 5½ in.; 3 to 4 in. later. Sepals, six, obovate, broad and blunt tipped with margins and apex curved back. Deep carmine on opening, fading in centre to mauve while margins remain dark. Stamens creamy. Late May-September.

C. viorna (C). Eastern United States of America, 1730. Herbaceous climber to 6 or 8 ft. Leaflets, three, five or seven, their tips acting as tendrils. Flowers solitary, almost globular but for recurved sepal tips which give overall urn-shape. Sepals, four, very thick and succulent, ¾ in. long, dusky red. July-August. Seed heads green and conspicuous. Related to *C. texensis*.

C. vitalba, Traveller's Joy, Old Man's Beard (C). Europe (including Britain), North Africa, Caucasus. Rampant climber to 30 ft. Leaflets, five, coarsely toothed. Flowers 1 in. across in panicles. Stamens more prominent than the four sepals, all being dingy creamy-white with greenish undertones. Little or no scent. July-September. Seed heads woolly and conspicuous, persisting into winter.

C. viticella (C). Southern Europe. Vigorous climber. Leaflets, seven, further subdivided. Nodding purple flowers 1½ to 3½ in. across. Sepals, four, often recurved at margins. Six-inch-long, thread-fine pedicels (with foliar bracts) give graceful appearance to the shrub in bloom. July-September.

C. viticella elegans plena (C). Strong growing. Flowers 2 in. across, packed with sepals in a dense rosette. Soft 'old rose' purple. July-August. An old variety recently brought back into commerce through Mr Graham Thomas, to whom I am indebted for this note.

C. viticella rubra (C). Vigorous. Leaflets, seven. Flowers semi-nodding, 2½ in. across. Sepals four (or five), 1 in. wide, deep velvety-red, whitish at base. Styles very dark red, almost black. Anthers brownish. July-August. Often misnamed Kermesina and Royal Velours.

Vyvyan Pennell (B). Vigorous. Leaves ternate. Flowers form neat, fully double rosettes, 6 in. across. Frame of large lilac outer sepals. Cushion of smaller lavender-blue inner sepals. May-June. A few single flowers later. A cross between Daniel Deronda and Beauty of Worcester.

W. E. Gladstone (C). Not vigorous though capable of reaching 10 ft. Leaves simple or ternate. Leaflets large, up to 3¾ in. across and 6 in. long. Upper surface very shiny when young. Flowers up to 10 in. across. Sepals, six or seven, obovate, uniformly lavender. Stamens prominent; anthers purple. July-October.

White Moth (A). A selection of *C. alpina* var. *sibirica* (q.v.). Light, yellowish-green, biternate foliage. Flowers 2¼ in. across, white throughout with hint of green. Sepals 1¼ in. long, ½ in. wide. First row of four staminodes 1 in. long, projecting beyond sepals but very narrow; inner staminodes conspicuous and numerous. Hence a fat, fully double flower resembling *C. macropetala*, but smaller. Latest flowering of its group. May.

Will Goodwin (B). New. Pale lavender, with six very broad (2½-in.-wide) sepals, overlapping, corrugated, wavy margined. Contrasting dark stamens.

William Kennett (B). Vigorous. Leaves nearly all simple. Flowers 6 to 7 in. across. Sepals, eight, broad and overlapping, rough textured with crimped margins. Strong lavender-blue with reddish-purple central stripe on opening (far more marked than in Mrs Hope), gradually fading out. Dark purple anthers. May-June, August-September.

Xerxes. The true plant seems to be no longer in cultivation. Of recent years Elsa Späth and Mrs P. B. Truax have both been erroneously listed as Xerxes.

Glossary of Botanical Terms Used

ANTHER. The part of the stamen containing the pollen grains.

AXIL. The junction of leaf and stem. AXILLARY. Arising therefrom.

BIPINNATE. A leaf in which the primary divisions are themselves pinnate.

BITERNATE. A leaf divided into three parts which are themselves divided into three.

BRACT. A modified leaf growing near the flower.

CARPEL. One of the units of the female part of the flower.

CORDATE. Heart shaped.

CULTIVAR. A plant which has originated in cultivation.

DIOECIOUS. Having the sexes on different plants.

FILAMENT. The stalk of the anther, the two together forming the stamen.

FOLIAR. Leaf-like.

GENUS. A group of species with common structural characters. The name of the genus is, in designating a plant, placed first and has a capital initial letter.

GLABROUS. Without hairs.

GLAUCOUS. Bluish.

HERMAPHRODITE. Containing both stamens (male) and ovary (female) in the same flower.

LANCEOLATE. Narrowly elliptical, tapering at both ends.

NODE. A point on the stem where one or more leaves arise.

OBOVATE. Broadest above the middle (of a leaf).

OVATE. Broadest below the middle (of a leaf).

PANICLE. An axial flower stem along which the flowers are arranged on branching stalks.

PEDICEL. The stalk of a single flower.

PEDUNCLE. The stalk common to a branch of flowers.

PERIANTH. The floral leaves as a whole, including petals and sepals if both are present.

PETALOID STAMENS. Stamens which are petal-like in colour and texture.

PETIOLE. The stalk of a leaf.

107

PHOTOSYNTHESIS. The synthesis, made by the green plant parts, of sugar and starch from carbon dioxide and water, in the presence of daylight.

PINNATE. A leaf composed of more than three leaflets arranged in two rows along a common stalk.

PUBESCENT. Shortly and softly hairy.

SEPAL. One of the parts forming the outermost whorl of the flower.

SERRATE. Toothed like a saw.

SPATHULATE. Paddle-shaped.

SPECIES. A group of individuals which have the same constant and distinctive characters. The name of the species is, in designating a plant, placed second, and has a small initial letter.

STAMEN. One of the male reproductive organs of the plant.

STAMINODE. An infertile stamen.

SYNONYM (SYN.). A superseded name.

TERNATE. A compound leaf divided into three parts.

VARIETY (VAR.). A natural group within a species, occurring in the wild; normally given a name of Latin form.

WHORL. More than two organs of the same kind arising at the same level.

× The sign for hybridisation.

Index

The figures in parentheses refer to line drawings on the text pages. The Descriptive List of clematis in cultivation, pp. 89 to 106, is not included in this index as it is in alphabetical order.

109